I0175666

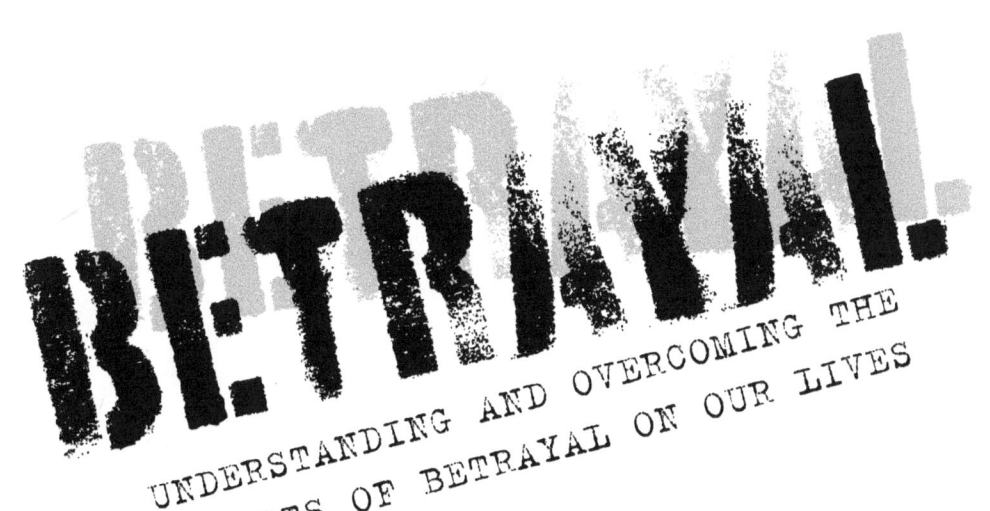

BETRAYAL

UNDERSTANDING AND OVERCOMING THE EFFECTS OF BETRAYAL ON OUR LIVES

FOREWORD BY
LUKE & SANDY WALTERS

UNDERSTANDING AND OVERCOMING THE EFFECTS OF BETRAYAL ON OUR LIVES

TERESA BRIDEAU

This book is protected by copyright laws of the United States of America. This book may not be copied or reprinted for commercial gain or profit. The use of short quotations or occasional page copying for personal or group study is permitted and encouraged. Permission will be granted upon request.

Scripture quotations taken from the Amplified® Bible (AMP), Copyright © 2015 by The Lockman Foundation. Used by permission. lockman.org

The Holy Bible, Berean Standard Bible, BSB is produced in cooperation with Bible Hub, Discovery Bible, OpenBible.com, and the Berean Bible Translation Committee. This text of God's Word has been dedicated to the public domain.

Scripture quotations marked (ESV) are from The ESV® Bible (The Holy Bible, English Standard Version®), © 2001 by Crossway, a publishing ministry of Good News Publishers. Used by permission. All rights reserved.

Scripture quotations taken from the (KJV) King James Version public domain in the U.S. Copied, used, and distributed freely.

Scripture quotations taken from the (NASB®) New American Standard Bible®, Copyright © 2020 by The Lockman Foundation. Used by permission. All rights reserved. lockman.org

Scriptures taken from the Holy Bible, New International Reader's Version®, NIrV® Copyright © 1995, 1996, 1998, 2014 by Biblica, Inc.™ Used by permission of Zondervan. www.zondervan.com The "NIrV" and "New International Reader's Version" are trademarks registered in the United States Patent and Trademark Office by Biblica, Inc.™

Scriptures taken from the Holy Bible, New International Version®, NIV®. Copyright © 1973, 1978, 1984, 2011 by Biblica, Inc.™ Used by permission of Zondervan. All rights reserved worldwide. www.zondervan.com The "NIV" and "New International Version" are trademarks registered in the United States Patent and Trademark Office by Biblica, Inc.™

Scripture taken from the New King James Version®. Copyright © 1982 by Thomas Nelson. Used by permission. All rights reserved.

Scripture quotations marked RSV are from the Revised Standard Version of the Bible, copyright © 1946, 1952, and 1971 the Division of Christian Education of the National Council of the Churches of Christ in the United States of America. Used by permission. All rights reserved.

Scripture quotations marked MSG are taken from The Message, copyright © 1993, 2002, 2018 by Eugene H. Peterson. Used by permission of NavPress. All rights reserved. Represented by Tyndale House Publishers.

Scripture quotations marked (TLB) are taken from The Living Bible, copyright © 1971 by Tyndale House Foundation. Used by permission of Tyndale House Publishers, Carol Stream, Illinois 60188. All rights reserved.

God
MANIFEST | PUBLISHING
www.GodManifestPublishing.com

This book and all other God Manifest Publishing books are available on Amazon.com.

Cover designed by Jonnathan Zin Truong
Interior designed by Jonnathan Zin Truong

For more information on foreign distributors, email publishers@godmanifestpublishing.com
Reach us at on the internet: www.godmanifestpublishing.com

ISBN: 979-8-9920028-7-4
eBook: ISBN: 979-8-9920028-8-1

Printed in the United States of America.
Copyright © 2025 Teresa Brideau.
All rights reserved.

CONTENTS

Acknowledgement 9
Foreword 11
Preface 13
Introduction 17
PART I: Understanding the Effects of Betrayal on Our Lives 25
    Chapter 1: A Matter of the Heart 27
    Chapter 2: So What's Wrong with Human Reasoning?.................39
    Chapter 3: Why Praise God..51
PART II: Overcoming the Effects of Betrayal on Our Lives 61
    Chapter 4: The Four C's 63
    Chapter 5: Unveiling Pride..95
    Chapter 6: Weapons That Prosper! 105
    Chapter 7: What's Faith Got to Do with It? 113

ACKNOWLEDGEMENT

In acknowledgment of the One who brought me out of the darkness and into His glorious light, He is the Alpha and the Omega, the Beginning and the End, the First and the Last. He is and always will be Faithful and True. To the One who loves and brings a living hope to billions of souls created by Him for His glory, it is to Him alone that I owe my life and acknowledge His goodness and mercy.

Thank you, Father, for Your invitation to holiness through the death, burial, and resurrection of Your Son. Thank you, Jesus, for my salvation, which has freed me to love and forgive. Your grace and truth are amazing! Thank you, Holy Spirit, for Your help, Your wise counsel, encouragement, and power to live a life worthy of my calling. I love You! There is no one like You. Thank you to every single friend and family member and foe for allowing me to experience the good, the bad, and the challenging times that drew me to seek, ask, and knock for the unadulterated truth of the Kingdom we were all created to enjoy for eternity.

I pray You reveal Yourself in a special way to every reader who is hungry to know You and desperate to trust in Your steadfast love for them. Heal and restore the souls of Your people, in Jesus's name. Amen.

FOREWORD

This work of the heart will go to the deepest hidden places to reveal how God wants ALL your hearts to be healed and free. Teresa opens her life journey's vulnerability to show how God can redeem one's soul from the treachery of betrayal. God flips the script from the torment and bitterness of the past to transform us into His beautiful, bright, shining ones in the darkness of this world.

As you lean into this work, allow God to stretch your capacity to receive His merciful goodness.

This book reminded me and my wife that it's never over with God. When the enemy has you cornered seemingly into "checkmate" *on the chessboard of life*, remember the King always has the last move!

As you work through this book, get ready for a momentum of the Holy Spirit to move you toward fulfilling His purpose for your life!

Daylight's Burning…

Luke & Sandy Walters
MAP 1040

PREFACE

"For I received from the Lord that which I also delivered to you: that the Lord Jesus on the same night in which He was betrayed took bread…"

1 Corinthians 11:23 NKJV

Several other passages in the New Testament verify that Jesus Himself walked through the painful experience of betrayal *(Matthew 26:23-25; Mark 14:18-21; Luke 22:21-22; and John 13:21-30 ASV)*.

In the Book of Psalms, David struggled with betrayal. "Even my own close friend in whom I trusted, who ate my bread, has lifted up his heel against me [betraying me]" *(Psalm 41:9 AMP)*. This seems to parallel John 13:18, where Jesus was referring to Judas who ate His bread, then lifted his heel against Him. An interesting thought here is even though Judas partook of physical bread at that table, he was also fed spiritual food when he walked with Jesus. What spiritual food am I referring to, you might wonder? Jesus calls Himself, "The Bread of Life." *(John 6:35)* He fed all those who followed Him with knowledge of the Kingdom of God. This knowledge [Bread] is eternal, and it is what sustains us throughout our lives in this world as well as the world to come. In Jesus's words, He says, "Do not work for the food that perishes, but for the food that endures to eternal life, which the Son of Man will give to you. For on him God the Father has set His seal" *(John 6:27 ESV)*.

During that intimate time with His disciples, Jesus introduced what would be a new and everlasting covenant in His blood, between God and mankind.

"And in the same way He took the cup after they had eaten, saying, 'This cup, which is poured out for you, is the new covenant [ratified] in my blood'" *(Luke 22:20 AMP)*.

He knew He was about to suffer excruciating pain in every area of His being. He also knew one of those at their Last Supper together was about to betray Him. "But listen, the hand of the one betraying Me is with Mine on the table" *(Luke 22:21 AMP)*. Jesus lovingly called him "friend" *(Matthew 26:50)*. He was a disciple who walked with Jesus throughout His ministry. He partook of this special Passover meal at least three times previously, with Jesus and the other eleven disciples. Sadly, Judas settled for a mere thirty pieces of silver in exchange for identifying the One who only showed him love. He may have walked alongside Jesus, but his heart was far from Him.

Recently, as I meditated on these Scripture passages in the Bible, I had to wonder why our Savior chose to be given up on the cross through the act of betrayal, and with a kiss nonetheless! *(Matthew 26:48-49)*. He could have just surrendered Himself to the authorities when He knew it was His time.

My own journey through betrayal caused me to run to Jesus, and over time, helped me realize that Jesus understands. He was with me throughout one of the darkest valleys of my life. He never left me. He will never leave you either. What a comfort and a blessing to know He understands. There truly is unspeakable joy in Christ Jesus. He is steadfast in His love toward us. He will NEVER betray us. Ever. It's who He is.

Could it be that Jesus loved us so much that He was willing to identify with this painful experience many of us humans go through? Or does it take on an even deeper meaning that would strengthen us and equip us to overcome the devastating effects of betrayal itself? These thoughts are what began the writing of this book you now hold in your hands. It is my prayer that you will open your heart and allow the Holy Spirit to reveal to you just how deep and how wide God's love is for you through the pages that follow.

The Bible shows us that God set eternity in every human being's heart *(Ecclesiastes 3:11)*. In other words, we were created for an eternal purpose! Eternal life is not temporary, but our human [physical] bodies are. So, there is much more we should be seeking after than just the here and now on planet Earth. In John 17:3, Jesus was praying to the Father and stated what eternal life is. He said, "And this is eternal life, that they know you, the only true God, and Jesus Christ, whom you have sent" *(ESV)*. The last part of verse 10 in Proverbs 9 says, "… the knowledge of the Holy One is understanding and spiritual insight" *(AMP)*.

Knowing our Heavenly Father is impossible without knowing Jesus. He explained to the disciples, addressing Philip's request for Jesus to show them the Father. "Jesus answered: 'Don't you know me, Philip, even after I have been among you such a long time? Anyone who has seen me, has seen the Father'" *(John 14:9 NIV)*.

What a blessing and a beautiful plan for God to send Jesus to this earth to model Kingdom living for each one of us. No matter what we are struggling with in this life, Jesus gives us the eternal solution. Know Him. God is love. Love is the answer.

Yes, God set eternity in YOUR heart. He created you to love and to be loved. This is why betrayal is so painful. It affects the very core of our purpose for being.

What a gift we have been given to know the Father's heart toward us through the unspeakable sufferings of His dearly beloved Son! I praise Him that the victory was won at the cross! I pray that understanding the process our Lord went through to get to that cross will be even more liberating to your soul! He truly does love you, as no one else can.

He went before us to trailblaze a path of hope, enabling us to partake of His Kingdom Life on earth as it is in heaven! Eternal life can begin here on earth by knowing Jesus personally. When our fleshly bodies return to dust, our new bodies will continue that relationship with God forever. The hope of heaven is deeply embedded within all of us. When we set our hearts to seek after Jesus, hope Himself; the anchor of our souls, He will be found. It's His promise.

Come with me as we explore His goodness toward you, the reader, and all of mankind!

INTRODUCTION

INTRODUCTION

Without a true understanding of how to walk in unconditional love, human relationships will most likely experience a negative impact from the things listed here:

Abandonment	Trickery	Rage	Lying
Rejection	Deception	Insensitivity	Discord
Manipulation	Prostitution	Slavery	Dissension
Lust	Selfish gain	Jealousy	Competition
Greed	Anger	Division	Entitlement
Envy	Control	Contention	Unforgiveness
Adultery	Hatred	Bribery	Mind games
Fornication	Criticism	Slander	Bitterness
Broken promises	Cruelty	Fear	Accusations
Shame	Injustice	Abuse	Emotional Stress

How many of these can you relate to? They are found in relationship dynamics that many times lead to betrayal, or they are the effects of betrayal. This is not an exhaustive list by any means. The words are intentionally displayed to create an awareness of just some of the manifestations of the human heart in need of restoration. Pride is at the root of the human heart. Only God Himself can purify our hearts. And indeed, He has made the way for us to achieve a pure heart, through Jesus Christ. If a pure heart were not possible, Jesus would not have said, "Blessed are the pure in heart, for they shall see God" *(Matthew 5:8 ESV)*.

There are many diverse types of relationships. The four main types of relationships are identified as **family relationships, friendships, acquaintanceships, and romantic relationships** *(assertbh.org.uk)*.

Unhealthy relational dynamics were not what God intended for man. Yet all of us at one time or another have experienced pain from many things listed here, as they are simply part of man's fallen nature.

Let's understand that according to God's Word, in the beginning, when man was created, God said His creation was "very good." This gives us a clue that these things listed above did not exist in the first-known human relationship between Adam and Eve until they were introduced to them by way of a sleazy serpent. The Bible identifies him as "more cunning than any beast of the field which the Lord God had made" *(Genesis 3:1 NKJV)*.

The Hebrew term here for cunning is "a'rum," which also means "prudent" or "sly" *(www.bibleref.com>genesis)*. In this context, the serpent here uses his craftiness with the sole purpose of destroying mankind's intimate relationship with his Creator. His dark intentions were (and still are) to ruin mankind.

This skillful, guile-filled perpetrator was able to trick the first human beings into believing they could dismiss God's instructions and choose for themselves what rules they would follow. He had to do it by cunning means. This serpent began to mess with their perception of God's Word to them. He was stirring doubt in their minds to change their focus. To get to the man, Adam, he chose to use the influence of Adam's wife, Eve, by lying to her first.

Eve chose to believe the words, "Did God really say...?" *(Genesis 3:1 NIV)*.

Doubt and unbelief led to her human reasoning, giving validity to the words of a serpent rather than to the words of her Creator God.

Sin is the "transgression of God's law" *(1 John 3:4 KJV)*. In other words, rebelling against God's rules for living. The sin wasn't in the temptation itself. It was in the action taken after choosing to give in to the temptation.

To put it another way, when we entertain thoughts and make decisions outside of God's rules, we are opening ourselves to every other type of influence opposed to God; we are availing ourselves to compromise—dismissing the one who alone has all the answers we need. Our decisions, as a result, are made against the source of all truth when we simply rely on human reasoning alone. The choices are in direct opposition to God's very nature. This is how the law of love is violated. Once that happens, compromise begins to operate in our thought process.

There is a term used today, called "gaslighting." It is a behavior that is utilized within a relationship to control another's thought process, thereby corroding the receiver's sense of certainty. It is one of many weapons used by the enemy of our souls to keep us in the place of doubt. If he can cause us to doubt God's words, our minds will begin to open to compromise.

His manipulation of our belief systems keeps many living in the Valley of Decision, always second-guessing what's right and what's wrong. Discernment is skewed. We subconsciously may even think uncertainty is normal. The lies manifest when we try to convince ourselves that it's impossible to know the Way, the Truth, and the Life. As the lies repeat themselves in our thoughts, they begin to play out in our lives; strongholds are built and become familiar.

Only Jesus can help us break the cycles that entangle us. He loves our souls. He died to set us free from the bondage of lies.

Back to the Garden. When Eve perceived what was said through deception, she entertained the lie until it led to action. "She took of its fruit and ate" *(Genesis 3:6 ESV)*. She ate from the tree of the knowledge of good and evil, the only tree in the entire garden that God instructed these two humans on earth not to eat from.

Based on Scripture, it seems that the serpent knew if he could get Eve to take her mind off God and change her focus to self, pride would have an open door to enter and strip her of the humility she walked in, openly communicating with God. It appears the enemy of God intentionally planned to cut off all communication between mankind and his Maker. If he could subtly get them to disobey and eat the forbidden fruit, he would have endless opportunities to influence them in their natural state of being while separated from God.

Sometimes, I like to think the forbidden thing eaten (in a spiritual sense) from the tree of the knowledge of good and evil was the word of the serpent; his word attached to the actual physical fruit that was taken.

Proverbs 18:21 indicates that death and life are both the fruits of your mouth. In other words, what you confess will either lead to death or lead to life. Adam and Eve chose of their free will to take and "eat" the words of the enemy. Everything that comes out of his mouth is death. He is a liar. The New International Version says it this way: Proverbs 18:21: "The tongue has the power of life and death, and those who love it will eat its fruit" *(NIV)*.

The fruit of the serpent's mouth was and is deadly. God told them they would die if they ate the fruit from that tree *(Genesis 2:17)*.

After the woman ate, she offered the forbidden fruit to Adam, and he ate. The serpent had imparted his very nature by the power of agreement. Pride moved into the human heart and caused Adam and Eve to betray their Maker. Thus, the serpent's nature was taken on by the first humans. In today's world, we seem to identify this as human nature. Human [carnal] nature is hostile toward God *(Romans 8:7)*. The reality is Satan's nature, through the serpent, was projected onto the first humans. Some may argue over whether the serpent was the devil in disguise. I would like to share a couple of thoughts regarding this argument.

First, when God created Adam and Eve on the sixth day, He called His creation, "very good." All the other previous days God was creating, "God saw that it was good" *(Genesis 1:4, 10, 12, 18, 21, 25)*. Secondly, we note AFTER this, a serpent appears on the scene. In Genesis 3:1, the Hebrew word used for serpent here is "Nahash." In the first book of the Torah, the serpent is portrayed as a deceptive creature or trickster, who promotes as good what God has forbidden and shows cunningness in its deception. *(en.wikipedia.org/wiki/Nahash)* When we consider this character trait, it is congruent with the very character of the serpent found in the Book of Revelation: "And the great dragon was cast out, that *old serpent, called the Devil and Satan*, which deceiveth the whole world …" *(Rev 12:9 KJV). (My emphasis in italics.)*

I'm aware that there are several thoughts on the issue of whether the serpent mentioned in Revelation is the same serpent that is described in the Garden of Eden. Regardless, the point I would like for us to understand is that neither of these serpents [whether dwelling on land or sea] was on God's side. Both are evil and against humanity having any relationship with Him. They are opposed to truth. They are deceitful. This is why I believe they are one and the same. As you study for yourself, you are free to come to your own conclusion.

One decision in the Garden of Eden left us all vulnerable to the darkness with no light to see God. His love, originally imparted to Adam and Eve at the time of their creation, was now covered up due to a free choice made by them [under the sway of the serpent]. Remember, they were made in God's image, in His likeness. They chose to disobey.

Looking at the list above now, can we see how these behaviors crept into relationships? Without God, generations have been blinded by pride in their limited knowledge and understanding. Humanity has since been deciding for itself what is good and what is evil. The entire foundation of man's decision-making was based on deception.

Eating this fruit was an act of rebellion against God [Love], whether it was intentional or not.

Fear and shame immediately followed, as you can read in the third chapter of Genesis. They were already deceived into thinking that God couldn't see them if they hid from Him. Fear, fueled by shame, became present in their souls. Verse 10 says, "I heard you in the garden and I was afraid because I was naked, so I hid" *(NIV).* The nature of Adam and Eve had already become perverted. The evidence shows up in the blame game that took place in the garden when God asked Adam and Eve who told them they were naked. The confrontation did not go well. Sin had separated them from their Creator. Adam and Eve no longer felt a sense of accountability to the One they had been communing with daily. They would now rely on each other's feelings; each one's perception of themselves.

Their perfect world began to fall apart, removing them from their eternal source of life; A life filled with love, joy, peace, harmony, and abundance. They would now be living a life separate from God's fullness; no longer believing His best for them. They would now begin to experience life without faith in Him and His power; no longer allowing God to breathe purpose and truth to them. Without God's breath, true life ceases to exist.

So, what about the origin of the serpent in the Garden? This subject will be discussed later to help us understand how our thoughts can be challenged by outside influences.

PART ONE

UNDERSTANDING THE EFFECTS OF BETRAYAL ON OUR LIVES

CHAPTER ONE
A MATTER OF THE HEART

History notes betrayal operating in every sector of life: the marketplace, the political arena, churches, the educational system, the courts, the entertainment world, and even in our own homes and families.

Betrayal severs relationships.

It's no wonder that there is so much pain in the world today. Jeremiah 17:9 describes the human heart when it is void of God's love:

Jeremiah 17: 9-10: "The heart is hopelessly dark and deceitful, a puzzle that no one can figure out. But I, God, search the heart and examine the mind. I get to the heart of the human. I get to the root of things. I treat them as they really are, not as they pretend to be" *(The Message).*

I know this is not popular, but to help us understand why we see so many problems in relationships today, it would be wise to search out the heart of all hearts—the Creator of mankind, God Himself.

I encourage you to go back and read those two verses again.

Many years ago, when I first saw this passage of Scripture, I thought to myself, "Oh no, that couldn't possibly be referring to me as I never killed anyone or robbed anyone or committed adultery, etc. ... I'm nice to people that I meet on the street. A heart that is 'hopelessly dark and deceitful?'"

Something in me didn't like to see these words printed in a book that was still yet to be tested for its authenticity in my life. That "something in me," I later learned, is called the pride of my own understanding. Let's be honest. Knowledge is power. When we understand the information given to us and share it with others, there is always the opportunity to become prideful. We must remember that God created our minds to think and receive information. He gives us the ability to understand. The Word of God is the foundation of pure knowledge *(Proverbs 30:5).* We need to give the Designer of our brains the credit [Glory] for our ability to think and reason.

The Bible says that God will honor those who honor Him *(1 Samuel 2:30).* Proverbs 29:23 says that "a humble spirit will retain honor"

(BSB). To be humble is to know the One from whom knowledge and understanding are drawn. Jesus is the WORD. He is all-knowing. He is the One from whom ALL blessings flow. One of those great blessings is giving us the ability to understand knowledge. He made us in "His image". We are created to get knowledge and understanding. We are also instructed in James 1:5 to ask for wisdom in how to use the knowledge we obtain. Nonetheless, in our getting, we are to remember who gives it all. James 1:17 informs us that "every good and perfect gift is from God" *(NIRV)*. Knowledge, understanding, and wisdom are all gifts. We should see them as such. We have a God who is pleased when we come to Him for these things. It brings Him honor.

He is the Creator. We are His workmanship.

Growing up, the Bible was something that sat on a shelf in my family's living room for decoration. I was raised to be a devout Catholic and attend church every Sunday. I knew that Jesus died on the cross for sinners. I knew that He came to the earth as a baby, wrapped in swaddling cloth. I had a lot of head knowledge about these things.

I remember when I was nine years old, I asked my mother if she would take that "big book" down from the shelf for me to read. I was determined to read it from cover to cover. I barely got as far as Genesis 2. I couldn't understand what I read, so I closed it up and began to rely solely on what the priests and other adults in my life would say about God.

I wanted to know where God came from, so I asked my mother one day as she stood there in the kitchen washing dishes, "Mom, where did God come from?"

I'll never forget her answer, which came with such confidence and boldness. She said without wavering, "Honey, you just have to believe that God was and is and always will be." As a young girl, I couldn't comprehend what my mom said, but somehow, I knew deep down what she said was right. From that point on, I just always believed it. I can say I knew about God but didn't know Him personally.

Fast-forwarding to August of 1982, at the age of twenty-five, I had an encounter with Jesus when I was alone in my living room and crying out to know Him. I wasn't finding answers to my life's questions through my religion. I sensed there had to be more. I was a young mother of two children at the time and had been married for five years. I loved my husband and children, but I still felt an emptiness inside. While the children were napping, I turned on the TV, which was a rare thing for me in those days. A Christian network called Daystar was on. The man talking was sharing about the love of God and how desperately He wanted a relationship with us. It was like this guy was listening in on my prayers or something. I wanted a relationship with God. I wanted to know Jesus personally. He led the listeners in a simple prayer of faith. I acknowledged that I was trying to do life without God and confessed my sins, asking God to come into my life and forgive me. I remember asking Him to help me to know Him. Upon receiving Jesus Christ as my personal Lord and Savior, I opened the Bible once again, and this time, I felt as though the words I read were directed straight at me.

My eyes fell on Matthew 7:7: "Ask and it will be given to you; seek, and you will find; knock, and it will be opened to you" *(ESV)*. Whoa! It was like God was personally telling me to ask Him for things, to seek Him, and to knock on the door of His heart with my questions. I felt loved and honored that He would want to take the time to teach me through His Word. His Spirit was beginning to open my eyes to understand! *(Luke 24:45; Ephesians 1:18)*

It was also during this time that I discovered the Scripture mentioned earlier in this chapter, Jeremiah 17:9. I didn't yet know what it was going to cost me as I began to step out of everything that seemed familiar to me. Suddenly, the belief system I had developed since birth and all the human reasoning I took pride in was being challenged by the words I began to read in this book called the Bible! This was merely the beginning of what has become the most exciting journey I have ever known!

What I mean is that I began to make decisions based on what I read in the Bible. My everyday life had a fresh outlook. I started asking God to show me His heart in how I was to treat people, especially when they were less than kind to me. I wanted more than anything to see the world as He saw it.

Taking His Word literally, without yet knowing the Holy Spirit [whom we need to reveal the heart of the Father through reading His Word], led to my walk becoming legalistic. Thankfully, He was there every step of the way and straightened me out as I continued to seek, ask, and knock. When I learned of the precious Holy Spirit, I was able to receive understanding because of my hunger for more of the things of God. Grace was a revelation that seemed to cascade like a waterfall in my soul! Sweet freedom began to come after me! It has been a journey of *faith, trust, and restoration.* I'll never stop seeking, asking, and knocking. I encourage you as well, to never stop.

This process of seeking, asking, and knocking, is what keeps my relationship with the Lord Jesus alive and refreshing. Through many hardships, I have found His Word to be true. I have found Him to be faithful. Through this process, I know I can trust Him. There is nothing like abiding in God's presence. It is the GREATEST BLESSING we as humans will ever walk in. When Galatians 5:16 says, "Walk in the Spirit," God is telling us to walk in His presence.

He empowers us with that amazing choice once we make Him the Lord of our lives. Choosing to do life WITH Jesus *is the way* to complete freedom from our sinful nature. My old way of thinking may not like it, but I am a "new creature" in Christ *(2 Corinthians 5:17),* who can understand how real love operates according to the Scriptures!

When I surrendered my heart to Jesus, I wanted to learn how to love as He defines it in the Bible. With His help, I was able to begin the process of releasing my old junky thinking to God. It is a lifelong, continual process, but it has gotten easier! Like anything in life, we must discipline ourselves. A habit must be created to catch our thoughts and ask ourselves whether those thoughts are edifying to our souls or going to bring us down. We have the power to acknowledge those thoughts before God and release them to Him. It's like assessing any potential damage before it occurs. Since thoughts bring actions, it is wise to prevent damaging actions by causing every thought to obey *love's way*. God can handle thoughts that seem overwhelming to us. He is pleased to take them from us as we surrender them. There really is POWER in saying no to the things of this world. This is evidence that God's grace is working in us to transform us!

Thank you for sending Your Holy Spirit to help us do that, Lord!

Surrendering our hearts and minds to Christ is not just a one-time, fix-all conversion moment. The process simply begins when we receive Jesus Christ into our hearts. Philippians 2:12 says we are to work out our salvation with "fear and trembling". That would begin by practicing, "taking every thought captive to the obedience of Christ" *(2 Corinthians 10:5 NASB 2020)*.

We are a work in progress. The good news is that God has given every one of us the tools to work out our salvation. We will discuss some helpful tools to overcome the effects of betrayal in part two of this book.

Faith is what pleases God, but it must be combined with works. James 2:26 says that faith without works is dead. To clarify my point here, I am not saying we are saved by our good works. The grace of God only saves us through faith in Jesus Christ. Then, by that very precious grace, our works are what we do in response to God's Word in our lives. We will find ourselves walking in obedience to the things He tells us to do, not because we have to but because we want to. Our love for our Creator is what will fuel the faith that will be living and active! As we grow in God's grace and knowledge, the daily choices we make will no longer be based merely on our human reasoning alone but will be founded on the Word of God. His Spirit in us will be our guide. This is called being transformed by the renewing of our mind *(Romans 12:2 NASB)*. It is when we allow ourselves to be led by God's Holy Spirit!

What I find to be so exciting is that the Bible says when we surrender our way of living to God and repent for living outside of His belief system, He gives us the very mind of Christ, His Son! I believe that more today than I did when I started this new life in Christ forty-three years ago. I've been experiencing His grace in so many ways. He gets all the credit for empowering me to walk out a life of obedience. Please understand that walking out a life of obedience will never go perfectly on this side of heaven but the gift of Jesus, who was and is perfect, will light our path. Much trial and error will hopefully keep us seeking God's help through the Holy Spirit inside of us.

When we stop asking God what He thinks about our behavior, when we stop seeking His wisdom, understanding, and knowledge about our lives, and when we stop knocking on the door of His heart, we enter dangerous territory, called compromise. In other words, we lose that "awe," that fear of the Lord, which opens the door to presumption.

King David knew this all too well, as he prayed to the God of Heaven, "Keep back your servant also from presumptuous sins; let them not have dominion over me! Then I shall be blameless, and innocent of great transgression" *(Psalm 19:13 ESV)*.

King David was a man with great authority who ruled over all of Israel and seriously sinned, yet he was documented as having a heart after God's own. That meant he recognized whose authority ruled over his heart. So, we as followers of Jesus Christ must have the same heart cry. When we surrender to our Maker, we are giving Him all authority over our thoughts, words, feelings, and actions. Too many times, we surrender to our old nature (where we are the "boss") and make choices without asking God first. Do we care in that moment if it's what He would desire? Not necessarily, if we are only led by our five senses that fuel our human reasoning. Thus, we are now in the land of presumption, assuming God will bless us for the choice we made. This human reasoning, many times, goes back to eating the fruit from the tree of the knowledge of good and evil. Please don't misunderstand. We are justified in Christ at the time we give Him our lives. But the working out of our salvation with fear and trembling is what cultivates holiness in us. This way, a true believer in the sacrifice of Jesus will also recognize that it is only by His grace and mercy that we can keep from presumptuous sins. Knowing the God of our salvation is like eating from the Tree of Life. Only through Jesus can we know God. He alone is the Way, the Truth, and the Life. Jesus is the only one who brought grace and truth to the earth *(John 1:14, 17 ESV)*.

Grace should NEVER become an excuse to sin. It is there as a supernatural gift to help KEEP us FROM sinning. God's grace will lead us to hate the sin in our lives. Notice, I didn't say it would cause us to hate ourselves. The enemy is right there to manipulate and deceive us into thinking we are to identify with the sins we commit. We belong to Jesus. Period. But God does expect us, as His children, to repent of the sin so that we are free to live out our identity in Him. We must turn away from it and turn wholeheartedly back to God. Talk about His mercies! Wow. And they're "new every morning" *(Lamentations 3:23 NASB 2020)*.

When King David's sins were exposed, he was quick to repent in the name of the One who has ALL authority! Are we quick to repent when the Holy Spirit shows us something in us that we may not be aware of? Are we brave enough to ask the Holy Spirit where there may be blind spots in our soul that need cleansing or correcting? Repentance brings freedom in Christ. The freer we get as believers, the faster we will be able to recognize what disappoints our Heavenly Father and turn from it quickly! The fear of the Lord will keep us from presumptuous sins and all other transgressions. We must obey God's commandment to walk in the Spirit. If we obey this one command, trusting He is always with us to help us, He says, we will not fulfill the lust of the flesh *(Galatians 5:16)*. Combine that with "For nothing will be impossible with God" *(Luke 1:37 NRSV)*. Let's allow ourselves in this way to go from faith to faith and glory to glory. That glory will reflect Christ's holiness on the inside of us, shining brightly to others, as we do His will and good pleasure, walking in the fear of His Majesty!

God's grace is sufficient, and in due time, we will reap the benefits as we allow God to transform our thinking. The sooner we surrender to the process, the sooner our transformation will take place. We will find ourselves living our lives reflecting the character of Jesus on the earth.

Why would we want to change our thinking to God's way? Do you want everything God has for you? Do you want to know what His good, acceptable, and perfect will is for your life? Would you like to understand and, more importantly, overcome the effects of betrayal and other negative things in your life? It won't happen unless your mind is renewed. Jesus paid the price for it, so why not?

God has a planned purpose for your life. He says so in Jeremiah 29:11.

If you lose your life for His sake, He will cause you to regain it for His purposes, but if you choose to keep living the way you find familiar since birth, without Him, you'll lose everything you could have experienced in this life and the life to come *(Paraphrased from Matthew 10:39)*.

The Gospel [Good News] of the Kingdom of God was made possible for you and me through the death, burial, and resurrection of Jesus Christ, God's only begotten Son! The first step is to BELIEVE He means what He says. Again, this is only the beginning of our mind renewal in Christ. Take Him at His word.

Proverbs 23:7 says, "For as he thinks in his heart, so is he" *(NKJV)*. We are renewing our minds to think as our wonderful Savior thinks when we read and study and spend time in His Word, the Bible. Ask His Spirit to lead you and guide you into all truth. He will do it! That's His part. Our part is to obey and surrender to His truth when He leads and guides us to it.

Yes! You are worthy of God's love, or Jesus would not have come to the earth to save you! He desires more than anything for you to believe Him so that you can walk freely in His unconditional love. When we're grounded and established in this type of love, we will experience peace like no other. God's peace can only come from seeking and pursuing it. *(Psalm 34:14; 1 Peter 3:11 NKJV)*

In other words, we really can't go after God's peace without pursuing Him. The two go hand in hand.

It is amazing to have peace that is too wonderful for words! It is beyond human comprehension! God's ways are above our ways!

I worked in a school system that promoted the concept of "filling one's bucket." This means that someone does or says something to make you feel valued and special; a way of affirming and appreciating you. I can only say that when I feel the most filled up is when I am walking in this precious *love and peace* that only God Himself can impart to me and through me. He is the real "bucket-filler." And He desires this for all of us! That is why Jesus came. He is LOVE. He carved out love's path on earth to show us what it looks like. He demonstrated that love "bears all things, believes all things, hopes all things, and endures all things" *(1 Corinthians 13:7 ESV)*. It is critical to understand this if we desire to be set free from the things listed in the earlier section of the Introduction.

Jesus was abused verbally, emotionally, and physically, so we are not to think He doesn't understand our situation. He will walk with us through every form of abuse with deep compassion. He is there in our struggles. He is our hope in every circumstance. He may direct us to leave the situation so that He can heal and restore our hearts. In many cases, that may look like Him guiding us to a Holy Spirit-filled and led counselor. He is faithful to heal the brokenhearted. He hears the cries of our hearts. He will lead the way! Trust Him. He will never betray us.

When we are filled up with love [God], there is no room for negative thoughts to stay around. Here are some wonderful Scripture verses that have become an anchor to my soul. I speak these blessings over myself and others often:

Ephesians 3:16-19 "that He would grant you, according to the riches of His glory, to be strengthened with power through His Spirit in the inner self, so that Christ may dwell in your hearts through faith; and that you, being rooted and grounded in love, may be able to comprehend with all the saints what is the width and length and height and depth, and to know the love of Christ which surpasses knowledge, that you may be filled to all the fullness of God" *(NASB)*.

Betrayal would not remain as a devastating effect on us if we were filled with love daily and really knew the One who defines us. People and/or our circumstances don't define us. God alone defines us as His sons and daughters. We just need Him to help us peel off our false selves that we've been programmed to believe since our physical birth on the earth.

The work of every believer in God the Father and His Son Jesus Christ is to put off the old (without God—our human reasoning) and to put on the new (with God—His spirit of truth).

Pray with me, if you will, Psalm 51:10 *(ESV)* "Create in me a clean heart, O God, and renew a right spirit within me." Praying God's Word over ourselves, shows Him we are willing for Him to transform us.

Heavenly Father, help us to renew our minds. Change our thinking to line up with Your heart. We need Your Holy Spirit to do the work in us. In Jesus's name, amen.

CHAPTER TWO

SO WHAT'S WRONG WITH HUMAN REASONING?

Human reasoning is an amazing thing.

Let's use this familiar example:

When we see fruit on a tree, we may want to eat it based on its outward appearance. When we inspect it, we feel for bruises or soft spots and may even smell it to see if it is fresh or ripe enough. Ahhh, finally we taste it to determine its sweetness! Oh yes, hear that lovely crunch. We eat the fruit from the tree without questioning the roots that were nurtured to produce that fruit. This is because the root is the unseen part of the process. **What we can't see is usually what is never assessed.** In other words, humans tend to walk only by what we see, feel, smell, taste, and hear.

Please bear with me in the simplicity of this fact:

Science has taught us to assess everything by our five senses. This assessment process is our human reasoning, which is a gift from our Creator. He knew how to knit us together in our mother's womb *(Psalm 139:13)* so that after birth we would be able to navigate our way in life, exploring the world around us through our five senses.

The sense of smell alone is mind-boggling! Science suggests that humans can discriminate among one trillion different odors. (Not a typo here. That's a trillion!) *(livescience.com)*. We are indeed fearfully and wonderfully made.

This is great if faith in our physical senses alone could lead to lasting love, peace, and happiness. If the foundation of love in our human relationships was meant to be led strictly by our five senses, then something is not working. When we research statistics on divorce rates and wars among nations and people groups, we see more brokenness than we may care to admit. When we rely solely on ourselves, we are being controlled by human reasoning through these five senses.

In his quote, Martin Luther put it this way: "All our experience with history should teach us, when we look back, how badly human wisdom is betrayed when it relies on itself" *(quotefancy.com)*.

There must be something outside of our wisdom, knowledge, and understanding that would fulfill our deepest need to love and to be loved.

The world has been experiencing the fruit of betrayal without understanding where its roots began. According to Matthew 7:18, a good tree cannot produce bad fruit. A bad tree cannot produce good fruit. A tree would be determined as good or bad depending on the root system and how well those roots have been nurtured. When the Bible mentions the word "fruit," it indicates something that is produced through the process of cultivation. Just as in the natural world around us, where various fruits are produced, so in the spiritual world (that is unseen and just as real), various fruits are produced. Science even teaches us the law of cause and effect. Fruit, being the finished product, so to speak, is a result or "effect" of a cause or "root" that began producing it.

What is the fruit of your life? In other words, how are you living your life, and what are the results of the choices you make in relationships that have come and gone through the years? Take a few moments to pause and think back. For some of you, this will take a lot of courage. Many would choose to go into denial about relationship issues as they are too painful to bring up. I know. I did for years. Choosing ignorance (even if subconsciously) will NEVER bring healing. At least, that's my experience.

When you know you are healed in your heart, you'll remember relationships without feeling the pain connected to them. Peace will have replaced the feelings of animosity and retaliation. Forgiveness and mercy will be felt toward that person or group of people rather than criticism and judgment.

If healing is still needed to bring joy back into your life, then be encouraged to know that Jesus took all your heart's pain and shame so that you could overcome every single event that pulled you down and made you feel worthless. Invite Him into your life's journey, and He will gladly show you the "root" of that fruit in your life. This is not an easy subject, as it demands that we go deep into the parts of our inner man. But God is well able to help us!

What is our "inner man?" This book attempts to focus on bringing a greater awareness of our inner self ... the part of us that cries out for our destiny. That place in us that has an intense desire to understand life and its purpose; those deep passions within us that cry out to be manifested [brought forth] somehow in the earth.

God created us to love and to be full of joy! How can we know this? It's not to be based on any man's opinion. It must be what God says in His Word. He is the Creator, so we must search out His heart toward His creation. I am learning more each day that when I surrender my thoughts to Him, He shows me things in His Word like:

"You make known to me the path of life; you will fill me with joy in your presence, with eternal pleasures at your right hand" *(Psalm 16:11 NIV)*.

"The precepts of the LORD are right, giving joy to the heart" *(Psalm 19:8 NIV)*.

These are keys to finding God's joy! He is the One who makes our path of life known to us! He is the One who fills us with joy when we are in His presence! When we get to know His heart, His joy will spill into ours! We must choose to surrender our old nature so we can put on our new one! *(Ephesians 4:22-24)*.

Surrendering is dying to our selfish ways. It's choosing to continually give up our thought patterns and reasonings that are opposed to God. When we do this, the result [fruit] is inevitably a love and joy that can only come from Him! It's so important to spend time with Him by reading His Word [with listening ears] and just talking to Him. Again, when we are in His presence, there is fullness of joy! Why wouldn't we want that?

We were made in His image. In Chapter 5 of the Book of Galatians, *love and joy* are listed as traits of God's character, among seven others.

If we want to be free from bad fruit in our lives, we will have to dig out the root that was saturated with poison to produce it! If we believe we were "made in God's image" *(Genesis 1:27)* and "God is love" *(1 John 4:8, 16)*, then we must change something that crept in to alter that state of our being. We must desire to search out this matter if we want to walk free from the bondage our souls were born into. God planned our restoration from the foundation of the world. He is bringing us back to Himself and surely calling it, "very good."

I don't know about you, but I desire from my innermost being to produce good fruit in my life. I want to be blessed to be a blessing. I want to nurture the root to bear the fruit I was created to bear. I pray that we are ready to do what it takes to walk in the fruit of the Spirit of God who made us.

Let's go back to Galatians. We find the fruit of God's Spirit, illustrating His character. In Galatians 5:22-23, we see, "love, joy, peace, patience, kindness, goodness, faithfulness, gentleness, and self-control" *(ESV)*. Of and by our own human reasoning and efforts, this fruit is impossible to walk in, but "With God, all things are possible!" *(Matthew 19:26)*. I like that … "But WITH God" (emphasis by me). Herein, I believe, lies the foundation of all knowledge; knowing that we need God to help us become all He has created us to be. We need real love to succeed in real relationships. We need to look outside of our own understanding. We need God. He is love and He created us to partner with Him in our life's story.

I've seen many people achieve highly acclaimed positions without God, and at the same time, they are not among the happiest either. There is still discontentment—a yearning for more. They have attained status according to the world's standards, but still, there is an emptiness—a void that needs filling. They've realized that wealth and riches without a real purpose of how to handle them lead to a dead end.

There is a profound Bible verse that has resonated with me for years, and that is, "God has set eternity in the hearts of men" *(Ecclesiastes 3:11)*. No matter how far we go in life, if God is not our partner in the journey, eventually, we will hit a dead end. For, "There is a path before each person that seems right, but it ends in death" *(Proverbs 14:12; 16:25 NLT)*. Notice it will seem right. That may be because we are leaning on our own understanding, without God's input.

The Bible says that God is "a rewarder of those who diligently seek Him" *(Hebrews 11:6 NKJV)*. This tells me that as I choose to diligently go after the One who holds the key to my reward, it must not be in a way that "seems" right to me in the natural way of thinking and reasoning! The Bible says that God is Spirit, and those who worship Him or seek Him MUST do it in *spirit and truth*. This is the ONLY WAY to find the True God that Jesus Christ taught about when He walked the earth as a man. Every other "seemingly right way" is counterfeit and will lead to discouragement and emptiness in the end. Even worse, the counterfeit brings deception, which results in eternal separation from a loving God who calls us to know Him, the One and Only God of the universe.

I'm reminded of another verse that says, "For My thoughts are not your thoughts, nor are your ways My ways,' says the Lord" *(Isaiah 55:8 NKJV)*. I found that this verse was a hard one to swallow because we humans have a lot of pride in our own understanding and human reasoning. Oh, did I say pride? That seems to be something the world looks at as a good thing in many ways. How many times have we said, "I'm so proud of this and so proud of that" or "I'm proud of who I am and what group of people I am a part of?" Wait a minute, what is so wrong with identifying with what we think is something to be proud of? We will discuss more on this subject later.

Let me gently remind the reader and myself as well that without God, it is impossible to see anything wrong with our own understanding. Without His help, we only have our natural senses to lean on. From the time we are born in this fleshly body, we are only trained to operate by what we see, smell, taste, feel, and hear. This is why once we are introduced to anything outside of this natural realm, it becomes a very sensitive and controversial subject.

Notice, though, that most, if not all of us are intrigued by things that are equated to being spiritual in nature. For instance, books such as the popular *Harry Potter* series and movies such as *Poltergeist, Twilight,* and even more recently, *Evil Dead,* have something in them that seems to strike man's curiosity about things outside of the natural realm. Since they are outside of our natural understanding, we choose to believe these things are merely something to entertain us, or we blow them off as fake or not "real." We may even think to ourselves, what a creative mind the writer has. This is usually as far as it will take us in our human reasoning.

The spirit realm does exist, and there are spirit beings that influence the writers of these books and movies. We will explore this truth later. The question arises as to why billions of dollars have been spent to engage ourselves in such "entertainment."

Based on the Scriptures, John 4:24 says, "God is Spirit." If God knew us "before we were even in our mother's womb," according to the book of Jeremiah, Chapter 1, and verse 5, this would indicate we had to be composed of a different essence before He formed us in the flesh, before our birth on the earth. Things of the spirit are part of our origin in God. Deep inside of us, there is a curiosity to learn of things that add super to our natural existence. Whether we choose to acknowledge those things as spiritual in nature or not, they still exist. Just like the law of gravity and other laws of nature, so there are spiritual laws. It is an entirely different belief system altogether! The Bible says that the human mind is enmity or hostile against God *(Romans 8:7)*.

In our human, natural state of mind, we are unable to understand things that are spiritual in nature. Most religions are aware that there are spiritual dynamics that somehow operate in this world but don't quite understand them. They just seem to be accepted as "phenomena." Our five senses are limited when it comes to explaining these types of things because this realm goes beyond our physical one.

When these things are not understood, our souls will usually choose to fear what is unknown. Fear plays out in so many ways, which can bring a lot of damage to the human heart and how it relates to God and others. Fear is the absence of trusting that God is in control of our lives in any given area. If we are left to only believe what our imaginations create without God in the picture, we are building mindsets and strongholds that are only enforcing our fallen nature. We would be setting ourselves up for a never-ending battle of always trying but never coming to a full knowledge of how to obtain peace within ourselves.

The Bible says, "God has not given us a spirit of fear, but of power and of love and of a sound mind" *(2 Timothy 1:7 NKJV)*.

In other words, if we are living in fear, we must know that God, who is love, did not give it to us. It comes from somewhere or someone else.

In that garden called Eden, the Creator shaped man from the earth itself, "the dust of the ground" *(Genesis 2:7)*, and breathed into him the breath of life. Man, at that very moment became a living soul (alive with a mind, a will, emotions, and passions). In other words, God breathed His very LIFE into you. He is Spirit. He gave you the power to believe, the power to choose, and the power to feel. Our soul plays out in the way we live on the earth, through our bodies. The soul part of us chooses to either obey our flesh nature (influenced by Satan) or God (who speaks through His Word and by His Spirit).

When the forbidden fruit was eaten, sin entered the world, separating us from God, separating us from the ability to intimately know Him. All that was available for us to make decisions was our nature without God's wisdom, knowledge, and understanding. This brought death to our spirits.

Praise God for loving us so much that He sent Jesus to pay the penalty of that death so that we could live again. This is what we, as believers in Him, embrace as a new birth! Being born again is living a life no longer separated from God, but once again, walking with Him and letting Him love through us! That's not just good news. That's GREAT NEWS!

Based on God's perspective then, the One who made us, we are spirit beings who have been entrusted with a soul and are housed in an earth suit, called a body. We are sent to the earth for a time, and according to God Himself, we will return to Him and take with us all that we have learned. Our bodies "will turn back into the dust of the earth again," but our spirit "will return to God who gave it" *(Ecclesiastes 12:7 NCV)*. Our spirit and soul will be given a new body that will not need natural oxygen and food to exist *(1 Corinthians 15:44)*. Our journey here and now on planet Earth determines our eternal existence. Jesus came so that our eternal existence could be with Him forever. He paid the ultimate price for us to live in God's presence for all eternity. We choose.

The only thing that would keep us from that life of paradise would be to reject Jesus and His teachings. He will not force us to choose Him. We must believe He is the only way to abundant life for all eternity. We are accountable to Him in this life and must choose His way of love. We are not promised tomorrow. The Holy Spirit is our helper and guide. We need to allow Him to show us God's way. I've heard several people ask that if God was so loving, then why would He allow people to live outside of paradise? Why would He send them to hell? God desires for ALL people everywhere to choose eternal life with Him *(1 Timothy 2:4)*, but He will not override the will of man. He is not a controlling, manipulative God. Man chooses whether he wants paradise (heaven) or hell (separation from God). Both places are real.

Human reasoning without God's guidance caused the fall of man as we can see in the Book of Genesis. Eve was using her natural senses to reason her way into eating the forbidden fruit *(Genesis 3:6)*. Rather than choosing to agree with the Wisdom of her Maker, she decided to "become wise" without God's help. Eve used her soul, which is comprised of her mind, will, emotions, and passions, to make that choice based on what she assessed in the natural. From that point on, man has been limited to making decisions separate from God. The forbidden fruit was not to be eaten, else she would "die" *(Genesis 2:17)*. In other words, knowledge of her true self, knowledge of her real identity in her Spiritual Maker, would cease to exist. There would be a separation/death, if you will, that would no longer allow her to connect with God. I am repeating this scenario in the garden intentionally, as it is foundational to our understanding of how our relationship was severed from our Creator, through the act of betrayal. When we make decisions as Adam and Eve did, based on a lie, **our own soul betrays who we really are in Christ.**

Adam listened to his wife's reasoning instead of the instructions of His Maker, thereby subjecting himself to the consequences of his disobedience as well. Adam and Eve gave control over to the natural part of their being in making that decision rather than the spirit part of themselves. This cut them off from the Spirit of spirits, God Himself. Prior to this act of disobedience, the Bible says that Adam and Eve communed with God. They were given dominion over every creature of the land, air, and sea. By not taking dominion over the serpent, they left themselves wide open to his cunning schemes. Disobedience caused a shift in the spiritual relationship they had with each other and between themselves and God. Adam and Eve's spirit was cut off from God. Thus, the master plan for mankind to love and be loved for all eternity was shunned by the first humans that were made. Humanity has followed in their footsteps ever since.

Thank God, as Creator of all that is seen and unseen, His love endures forever, and He has made a way to restore man's relationship, not only to Himself but between us humans as well! His body of believers, the Church, is the community by which we are gifted to grow in the grace and knowledge of our Lord and Savior. His Church, led by His Spirit, fitly joins all of us together and allows for an environment of support, prayer, and teaching of His Word. The challenge we all face to believe this, is to let go of our natural understanding and seek after God.

Our minds are miraculous gifts, but they were not meant to function without God's Spirit leading and guiding them. He is looking for a people who will once again commune with Him and agree with the way He chose for us to live according to His Spirit of love! He alone is worthy of our praise!!! This brings us to the next subject we will discuss. Praise and how it all ties into our original make-up.

Oh! We praise You, Lord! Keep putting new songs in our hearts for You!!

CHAPTER THREE
WHY PRAISE GOD

Psalm 139:14 reads: "I will praise you, for I am fearfully and wonderfully made; marvelous are your works, and that my soul knows very well" *(NKJV)*.

In the original Hebrew text, the word 'fearfully' *(yare)* here means "with great reverence and heartfelt interest and respect."

The word 'wonderfully' *(pala)* means "unique, set apart, uniquely marvelous."

WOW! No wonder the psalmist bursts out with exuberant praise in this verse. He realized the great love and "heartfelt interest" that went into his unique and very individually created being. Every one of us was created with intention and purpose by the hand of God in our mother's womb. You were uniquely formed. According to science, no one else on this planet has your fingerprint. Let that sink in. You were not an accident. God is perfect in all His ways. This means He is incapable of making mistakes. He purposed you to be brought forth into the earth, regardless of the circumstances that surrounded your birth. It's the enemy who hates our uniqueness in God's handiwork and who is constantly trying to mess with our self-image by speaking false identities to our minds. He will use anyone that we choose to listen to. Especially unsuspecting loved ones who don't yet know the Lover of their own souls. God loved us and accepted us, even if the mother that birthed us didn't know how to love us.

According to this Scripture, you truly are a masterpiece! The next time you are tempted to ask the Lord, "Don't you care about what is happening to me?" Remember this verse because the truth is, He does care for you and loves you with an acute intensity that cannot ever be measured. He loves you with an everlasting love!

So why is it that we don't feel this way much of the time? We find ourselves living day by day, paycheck to paycheck. We don't see ourselves as "fearfully and wonderfully made." How can we praise a God who says this about us when we don't see it in all the stress and fast-paced demands that are put on us in our daily lives?

What exactly is praise? This word has different meanings for some of us, so in using the definition in the context of this writing, it means:

"The extolling of a deity or the rendering of homage and gratitude to a deity" *(collinsdictionary.com)*.

In laying the foundation for this project, I felt it necessary to address the meaning of *"praise,"* as I believe it is an important aspect of our restoration to the Great Creator of the Universe, if not, THE most important aspect. We are reconciled to the Father through Christ, but our wounded souls are restored to wholeness when we fully embrace the power of praise. Please understand the great value in your heartfelt praise to the One who made you. Psalm 22:3 says that He inhabits the praises of His people! A soul longing for love, joy, and peace is a soul He promises to satisfy. He will fill your soul with goodness *(Psalm 107:9)*. Don't wait for everything in your life to "feel right" before you praise Him. He wants us to praise Him right where we are so He can come in and fill us with what we need.

Praising Him gets our minds off ourselves. It shifts our focus from thinking about the cares of this world and places our thoughts on God. It is an act of giving and showing love, as He defines it. Praise causes us to magnify the One who has all the answers to life's questions and allows us to see Him as far greater than any of our problems!

To break it down further, let's look at the word "extolling." This means "to praise lavishly; to exalt." To "render homage" is "the act of respect or allegiance to someone that takes an important position in one's life." This would mean putting this relationship with God first, above all other relationships. No other relationship should take the place of this most important one. By giving the highest priority to learning how to relate to God first, your other relationships will begin to reflect the love that is experienced between you and your Maker. Since God is love, He knows how to show that love through you to others.

Remember what happened in the Garden of Eden? That connection was lost because Eve listened to the voice of a serpent (deception) rather than the voice of God (Truth). We've all been given the ability to choose. God will not violate our free will, or it wouldn't be called as such. We choose.

In the New International Version of the Bible, the word "praise" is used 340 times. This act called praise is one of respect or allegiance to the Creator of the Universe.

Psalm 47:6-7 says, "Sing praises to God, sing praises; sing praises to our King, sing praises. For God is the King of all the earth; sing to Him a psalm of praise" *(NIV)*.

Psalm 69:34 declares, "Let heaven and earth praise him, the seas and all that move in them" *(NIV)*.

The creation was made to praise its Creator. Before man was created, the Bible shows us that angelic hosts, heavenly spirit beings, existed [and still do]. Let's study this, as the spirit world, which we do not see with our natural eyes, has had a great influence on us—perhaps without our awareness. Keep in mind, as mentioned earlier, what we can't see is usually what is never assessed.

In Job 38 and verses 4-7, God is speaking with Job and asking him if he was there when God laid the foundations of the earth "when the morning stars sang together, and all the sons of God shouted for joy" *(ESV)*.

We don't know how much time went by between God laying the foundations of the earth and creating man, but we do know that the angels were created first *(Read Job 38:4-7)*. Many places in Scripture talk of how the angelic hosts worship and sing before the throne of God *(Revelation 5:11)*. We also aren't told how many angels were created, but we do know that there are many—a great multitude! This could be in the trillions and beyond. We don't know. Man's standard of measure is nowhere near God's eternal standard.

The Bible speaks of one angelic being, whose name was Lucifer. Look at how he is described in the book of Ezekiel in Chapter 28 and verses 12-15: "You were the seal of perfection, full of wisdom and perfect in beauty. You were in Eden, the garden of God. Every kind of precious stone adorned you: ruby, topaz, and diamond, beryl, onyx, and jasper, sapphire, turquoise, and emerald. Your mountings and settings were crafted in gold, prepared on the day of your creation. You were anointed as a guardian cherub, for I had ordained you. You were on the holy mountain of God; you walked among the fiery stones. From the day you were created you were blameless in your ways---*until* wickedness was found in you." *(BSB)*

So, we can see here that Lucifer was a beautiful angelic being anointed and ordained by God as a guardian cherub. Picture him in your mind as a divine masterpiece created by God, full of splendor!! God only creates beautiful!! An artist expresses His heart when creating something. When that Creator/Artist is love, everything in His work will reflect that love. An artist will elaborate on canvas that which is impressed upon his heart. For mankind to be created in The Master God's image is too wonderful to comprehend! The Bible does not say that angels were created in God's image. It says that we are. Multiple billions of people on the earth, all intended to be expressions of their Master Artist's heart, bringing glory to His name. Angels were created to also bring glory to God. They were created to praise and worship Him and to serve Him in various ways.

How much more should we praise and worship a holy God who created us in His very own image?

Earlier in the book, I said we would discuss who that serpent in the Garden of Eden was and where he came from. Let's continue in Ezekiel to see what Lucifer did to change his glorious position in heaven.

The Bible tells us that Lucifer's heart began to change toward his Maker. He began to focus more on his own beauty, his own wisdom and gifts, than on the One who gave him all that he had. Lucifer began to lift himself up, rather than lifting the God who made him. When his mind turned away from God, corruption crept into his heart, and he began to lie to himself, thinking that he could be as powerful and all-knowing as God. Thus, deception was born.

Ezekiel 28:17: "Your heart was lifted up because of your beauty; you corrupted your wisdom for the sake of your splendor."

Lucifer's beautiful character had now become defiled. He could no longer call heaven his home. His relationship toward God within the boundaries of love was now broken. Thus, betrayal was imminent. This beautiful angel, Lucifer [which means "light bearer"], not only turned against His Maker out of self-deception and pride but also managed to turn one-third of the angels against God. The Bible says there was a war in heaven! The change of heart in a third of the angels led by Lucifer brought hostility. Turning away from God was a choice to turn away from love, joy, peace, patience, kindness, goodness, faithfulness, gentleness, and self-control. By choosing to reject all these things as a way of existence, God changed this light-bearer's name to Satan, which means "adversary." Satan was now ruler over those he led into rebellion against God. These angels were named demons.

God cast Satan and his demons down to the earth. Let's look at the book of Revelation in Chapter 12 and verses 7-9:

"And war broke out in heaven: Michael and his angels fought against the dragon, and the dragon and his angels fought, but they did not prevail, nor was a place found for them in heaven any longer. So, the great dragon was cast out, that serpent of old called the Devil and Satan, who deceives the whole world; he was cast to the earth, and his angels were cast out with him" *(NKJV)*.

Did you catch that? Within this text, we can see another name, which the enemy of God was given. It is the "serpent of old." Who then do you suppose the serpent was in the Garden of Eden spoken of earlier? Just as Satan swayed a third of the angels to turn away from God and look with pride upon themselves, so he is using the same evil strategies to turn unsuspecting humans away from truly knowing their Maker. He is the master betrayer and knows exactly how to tempt the sin nature in man that would lead to the very act of betrayal.

Revelation 12:9 reminds us that Satan does not play fair! He is after the whole world with his deceptive schemes. None of us are immune to them. The Garden of Eden is where the enemy stepped into mankind's realm to try and destroy the plans God has for him. Compared to all the beasts of the field that were created by God, this serpent brought with him the most vile and cunning nature to the Garden of Eden. This is why we need our precious Creator!

Jesus was sent to destroy the works of Satan in our lives. He allowed Himself to even experience the pain of betrayal so that through Him [Jesus], we would be empowered to overcome this deep wound in the human heart. The enemy's game is betrayal. He betrayed His Maker. He deceived a third of the angels to betray their Maker. He is continuing to cause many humans to do the same. Praise God that Jesus took that kiss of betrayal, canceling the devil's long-term plan, so you and I could be reunited with the Father for all eternity.

Love conquered betrayal's kiss.

Praise empowers us to reach out to God in adoration. To praise God is to show Him how we feel toward Him! It's the very least we can do, as He loved us first even while we were yet rebelling against Him. When we receive God's Son into our life, we are receiving our Creator. We are choosing to no longer live under the sway of pride, deception, presumption, hate, lust, and everything else listed in the Introduction of this book.

By praising God after making this lifelong decision, He will guide us by His precious Holy Spirit. He will literally transform us to His very nature of holiness—the nature Adam and Eve experienced before sin entered their lives. I will say it again. Praise keeps our focus on Him and off ourselves. God will let us see how He sees. He will make known to us His loving plans for us.

The enemy is on this planet for a while but not forever. The Bible says that there is a lake of fire reserved especially for him and his demons. In the meantime, with Christ in us, we will be able to overcome every obstacle that the old serpent may place before us. It's not easy. It's called PROCESS. And it's a long one. We will look more like our Lord as we surrender to the process. You and I are destined to rule and reign with Jesus Christ forever!! Does anyone want to praise Him right now with me? He is Wonderful, Counselor, Mighty God, Everlasting Father, and Prince of Peace!!!

If you have been betrayed and find it difficult to praise the One who made you, don't be discouraged. Where man has let you down, know this: Your Maker, who designed you, is incapable of betraying you. It isn't His nature. He wants you to know that He will never leave you nor forsake you, my friend. He is worthy of your praise. Your healing is just around the corner! You will praise again!! Trust God. Don't give up! He will turn your life around if you let Him. Nothing is too hard for Him. Nothing.

Sweet Jesus!! Thank you for being with me in the process. I praise you for never leaving me or forsaking me!

PART TWO

OVERCOMING THE EFFECTS OF BETRAYAL ON OUR LIVES

CHAPTER FOUR

THE FOUR C'S

A diamond is beautiful to behold. When displayed under a light, it becomes even more brilliant. A jeweler will tell you that the brilliance is a result of how the stone has been cut. The more facets, the more fire and brilliance! When light passes through, it reveals the full integrity of that diamond. In other words, light and magnification are needed to see the true color, cut, and clarity of the stone. An extremely precise scale is used to determine the carat of a diamond, which is its weight.

The value of the stone is made obvious after it is taken through an intense process. I was thinking about this illustration considering human suffering. Hypothetically, if we were to imagine ourselves as a diamond in the rough for a few moments, I wonder if we would see the full value of it, or perhaps even recognize it as a diamond. It may look to many of us like a piece of dull rock. The true beauty is hidden below the surface.

A skilled craftsman is aware of what is behind the outer surface. He knows the process is a delicate one but necessary to bring forth the full character and potential of that stone. His goal is to transform that cloudy piece of rock into its full potential of a stunning, breathtaking jewel! The master diamond cutter sees the sparkling stone in his mind's eye before ever starting the cutting process.

This is the same with our Master Creator. He sees our full potential. His intentions are never to leave us in the rough. There is a process we all must go through on this earth. The good news is that our God is right there with us! He is involved in every intricate detail of our life. As a matter of fact, He already sees us as His masterpiece, according to Ephesians 2:10 *(NLT)*. Interestingly, He inspired the Apostle Peter in 1 Peter 2:4-8 to liken believers as unto living stones, being built into a spiritual house; a holy priesthood.

Let's read from the heart of your Heavenly Father:

"As you come to Him, the Living Stone, rejected by humans but chosen by God and precious to him—you also, like living stones, are being built into a spiritual house, to be a holy priesthood, offering spiritual sacrifices acceptable to God through Jesus Christ" *(NIV)*.

He is transforming us by His Spirit so that the world will recognize the treasure inside of us. People will see that Jesus is the light shining in and through us. They will see our true selves flourishing in the light of God's love!

As we experience life, we will find ourselves enduring trials and hardships along the way. We might ask why, especially when our souls seem to be put under so much pressure. This is the very process we need to examine ourselves on the inside. Much like the craftsman working on the diamond, we could look at our trials and challenges in life as God "cutting" facets in our character. He refers to us as His handiwork in another translation of Ephesians 2:10. The result will bring about the brilliance of His Son within us as we surrender to the process. God already sees our great potential before we are even formed in our mother's womb. You are far more valuable than a diamond.

Let's look at Acts 14:22, where the apostle Paul was stoned and left for dead, yet continued to preach with the disciples in cities such as Lystra, Iconium, and Antioch:

"… We must suffer many hardships to enter the Kingdom of God" *(NLT)*.

Paul understood that opposition was going to be a part of the process in developing God's loving and merciful character. He didn't cower when faced with persecution. He continued to encourage the disciples to remain firm in their faith!

So, what does this have to do with betrayal? The greatest opposition we will ever face to growing in the grace and knowledge of our Lord and Savior Jesus Christ is ourselves. We are betrayed by our own sinful nature. The enemy knew this in the Garden of Eden. He hates God. He hates everything God created, especially, you and me because we were created in God's image. As mentioned earlier, when God breathed into the man, he BECAME a living soul. We were intended to walk with the Lord from the beginning. His love defines us for all eternity. Sin presented itself and slapped a false identity on us. Of course, we weren't aware of this as the world we were born into began shaping our identities without God's input as to who we really are. We aren't who we think we are. Sounds strange? It will to our natural mind. We've been conditioned to think our existence without God's guidance is "normal." Without God's breath, we never would have become a living soul, wrapped in a human body. Think about that.

Since that moment, Satan has been aggressively trying to steal our identity in Christ Jesus. And he continues to use anyone willing to speak a different identity into our lives. We have been told we were so-and-so and such-and-such since birth. We began to believe what the enemy was defining us as, through others.

Choosing to believe anyone or anything outside the parameters of our loving God is what creates a false identity. And false identities are drawn to false religions, which will seem familiar because our families for generations have walked the same familiar paths. It is choosing to believe a lie. Not only are we believing lies about ourselves, but pride is invited into our thoughts to make us feel good about some of these identities. This is all done over time and on a subconscious level. We wouldn't see it without God's help.

Pride in our own understanding when dealing with life and life's issues is laying out a welcome mat for the enemy, inviting him into our soul. Our perspective, most of the time, comes from our personal experiences in life. Many of them are painful ones. The enemy (remember the subtle serpent) would love to keep us locked up in an emotional prison where our hearts can grow stone cold. If he can get us to think from a hopeless perspective, then he is winning the battle for our souls. This is pretty much our position before meeting the Lover of our soul.

God is in the business of not only rescuing us from harmful, destructive thinking, but He deeply desires to restore us. By His precious Spirit, He wants to transform us into the beautiful jewel He sees in us. In Zechariah, the last part of verse 16 it says, "...as the flock of his people; for like the jewels of a crown they shall shine on his land" *(ESV)*. Unhealthy thinking will not allow us to see our true potential. Christ in us is our hope of glory! Therefore, we need to understand that our mind, will, emotions, and passions will have a process to go through to gain the Master Cutter's perspective on our journey.

Our thinking makes all the difference in the world as to whether we become who we are destined to be. Unless we first believe that our Maker will never betray us, we will not be able to move forward in our healing since He alone is our source of wholeness. Having a close relationship with our Healer will allow us to be more sensitive to His instructions, causing us to experience a different way of thinking and doing things. Trust is a major issue when we have been betrayed. God is loving, patient, and kind. He wants to help us build our trust in Him.

Betrayal left wounds and even scarring in my heart that needed healing. I was afraid of being rejected again. Now that I'm on the other side of these heart wounds, I want to share how you can be healed and cultivate healthy relationships.

You can have closure, even if those that hurt you are no longer alive. You can still confess the sin of holding on to the past, crucify it to the cross, and cleanse yourself by covering it in the blood of your Savior. I just let you in on what you are about to learn regarding the 4 C's!

The Bible says that no weapon formed against us will prosper *(Isaiah 54:17)*. Well, we need to know what these weapons against us look like so we can use the tools God has given us to overcome the effects of betrayal on our lives.

The Lord has been teaching me so much about diamonds and the four C's I've even enjoyed opportunities to sell jewelry. No doubt, He knew He would get my attention by revealing four C's to help me get free from the effects of betrayal on my life! He has a purpose for everything we experience. These have worked for me through the years, and I'm so excited that He is allowing me to share them with you. Let's apply these four C's and enjoy the results of doing it HIS way!

CONFESSION. It is the first of the four C's and crucial to our mind renewal process.

Until we even become aware of what it is we need to confess, there will be no confession.

In my case, I had a lot of hateful thoughts. **Hate is a weapon against us.** I hated who I was, I hated my life, and I hated not having answers to fix my misery. In that state of thinking, I found myself betraying others by breaking their confidence and looking for things in others to gossip about so that I would feel better about myself. And by the way … I had given my life to Jesus several years before this behavior started being brought to my attention. I may have been saved, spiritually speaking, but I sure had a wrecked soul that needed a lot of work! Can I just say that destructive thoughts lead to destructive actions? It is a never-ending vicious cycle. I was unable to find peace in that behavior. I was stuck. Sure, I professed I loved God, but at the same time, I was bad-mouthing His children.

Let's identify this right now as being double-minded. God says when we are double-minded, we are unstable in all our ways *(James 1:8)*. Ouch! When our thoughts are fickle, the words that come out of our mouths will reflect those thoughts. The Bible says that "out of the abundance of the heart, the mouth speaks" *(Matthew 12:34 ESV)*. I thought I was good at hiding it, but when it came time to seek the truth as to why I was so miserable (and at one point, suicidal), I saw this in the Book of James: "But no human being can tame the tongue. It is a restless evil, full of deadly poison. *With the tongue, we praise our Lord and Father, and with it, we curse human beings, who have been made in God's likeness. Out of the same mouth come praise and cursing. My brothers and sisters, this should not be" (James 3:8-10 NIV)*. This Scripture right here immediately began to convince me that I desperately needed the Holy Spirit's help.

I couldn't see this in myself even though others may have. Self-deception will keep us blind to what is truly going on inside of us. Through frustration and tears, I asked the Holy Spirit to show me why I wasn't feeling peace in my soul. I came to a place of desperation for God. I wanted to feel and know His heart. "How do You see me, Lord?" I would ask. These words in James, Chapter 3, began to open my eyes. I was done being stuck! I decided to do whatever it took to get out of the deep pit of despair I found myself in. I never saw myself as being what the world calls two-faced. I wanted to be real with God and with people. I wanted to be real with myself.

The truth stings, but I knew if I was going to allow God to cleanse my thinking and repair my damaged soul, I was going to have to become real with myself first. Yes, I could justify my anger, rage, and bitterness for what had happened to me. But at the same time, staying in that frame of mind was not allowing me to cultivate healthy relationships. I had to choose to take my focus off my betrayer and give complete attention to the One who could heal and restore every part of me. I needed emotional healing, and a victim mentality was keeping me in bondage. I needed God's perspective.

I knew it was going to take some confessions for starters. The Word of God instructs us to confess our sins, so that was my first step in this process of restoration.

1 John 1:9 says, "If we confess our sins, He is faithful and just to forgive us our sins and to cleanse us from all unrighteousness" *(ESV)*.

When I cried out to God for help, then He began to show me through reading His Word that my thoughts were not the way He wanted me to think. HIS thoughts were to be my replacement.

As part of my story, which I can share now without my blood boiling, I was in an unhealthy marriage with an unfaithful spouse for twenty-three years. I chose to stay in denial for most of those years and would drink wine excessively at times to try to cover up the pain in my soul. When I received a phone call eighteen years into the marriage from a woman that I never met from out of state, I learned the behavior of my husband was pretty much a lifestyle.

He had said five years into the marriage, [the first known betrayal I was made aware of] when I met Jane (name changed to protect the guilty) that it was only a one-time thing. He said he "played in the fire and just got burnt." Well, he just got caught is what I translated that to mean after seeing so many signs after that first exposure. I had given my life to Christ three weeks before everything came crashing down. I remember driving down the freeway thinking, "My marriage is on the rocks." When I realized it was a lifestyle, I was even more devastated, as I was trying to forgive him since the initial betrayal. I read in Matthew 18:21-22, "Then Peter came to Jesus and asked, 'Lord, how many times shall I forgive my brother or sister who sins against me? Up to seven times?' Jesus answered, "I tell you, not seven times, but seventy-seven times'" *(NIV)*. And so, for many years—at least ten years since seeing these Scripture verses—every time the anger, bitterness, and rage would begin to surface, I said, "I forgive him, Lord."

Hold on. I'm not that good of a Christian girl. The bitterness continued to build up in my soul to the point of wanting to just leave the planet, so I didn't have to feel the depth of pain anymore. Especially knowing this was affecting our three children. How many of you can relate to this way of thinking? I checked myself into the La Quinta Inn near my home and was going to lie down on the railroad tracks that ran alongside the hotel. I remember for the first time in my Christian life, getting real with God regarding all my emotions. Something I never thought I should do since negative emotions were not allowed to be expressed in my childhood home growing up. I remember yelling at God. I didn't care if the hotel walls were as thin as cardboard. I was outraged (like a spoiled brat) with God as I proceeded with these words: "I'm obeying Your word! I've been confessing for over ten years, 'I forgive him. I forgive him. I forgive him!' and it's not working!! I still feel all this anger in my heart toward him!"

The Lord is so precious. He allowed me to go on for about ten minutes screaming at Him. He waited for all that mess to surface so that I would be prepared for what was about to happen next. He asked me (yes, I heard His voice; this was an encounter I will never ever forget), "How many billions of people would you say are on the earth?" In a very ill-tempered way, I answered, "I don't know!! What does that have to do with anything? Maybe 8 billion. I don't know!" He then proceeded to tell me that every single one of those people betrayed Him. Spiritually, they all followed someone or something else when they were intended to be in a relationship with Me, including yourself. Oh! That hit me real hard when He let that sink in for a moment. He waited for just the right timing, and then I heard Him gently say, "But I forgave you." I got it. I burst into tears. I never realized just how forgiven I was. I had the head knowledge. The revelation hit me so hard, I threw my face into the ground and said I was so sorry. I remember thinking (maybe out loud even) that if Jesus forgave me and multiple billions, then who am I to hold anything against one human being? I repented. I confessed the sin of hanging on to unforgiveness, and suddenly, I saw a vision of a dark cloud leaving to my left. The Lord began naming everything in that cloud: "Anger, Strife, Envy, Bitterness, Rage, Jealousy, Hatred..." There was a pause after that, where I felt a gaping hole or an opening in my heart is the best way I know how to explain it. Then, like a Nike swish of light coming in from the right side of the room, the Lord sweetly said, "Now there's room. Room for My love, My joy, My peace, My patience, My kindness, My goodness, My faithfulness, My gentleness, My self-control." God delivered me that evening. I've never been the same since. I thank Him regularly for intervening in my life. Oh, how He showed me that even though I professed to love Him and served in every church fellowship I was a part of for eighteen years, with a smile on my face, I was wasting away on the inside because of a deeply wounded soul. It wasn't until I confessed the sin of unforgiveness and repented, that My dear Lord and Savior could deliver me. He already knew what was in there. I had to see it so I could surrender it to Him. He is so patient with us. How many years of misery could have been spared if I had only known it was as simple as a repentant confession? His love for me overpowered all the hatred I had toward myself and my betrayer. His love needs to rule our hearts to overcome the effects of betrayal on our lives. When His love rules, we are shown our sins so we can confess them to Him.

I will end this part of my story here, but the Lord had me give the marriage a grace period of five more years, giving my spouse time to repent. He chose not to, unfortunately. It's amazing how the Lord removed me from the marriage. I like to call it a holy separation. There was no violence whatsoever. I embraced God's peace throughout the many changes that began to take place. The richest part about going through such a dark time in my life was that I made Jesus my husband.

The sexual addiction is what dissolved the marriage, but in that trial period, I was able to make the Lord my husband, regardless of my circumstances. He brought to life and made real for me Isaiah 54:5: "For your Maker is your husband, the Lord of Hosts is His name; And your Redeemer is the Holy One of Israel; He is called the God of the whole earth" *(NKJV)*.

I desired more than anything out of a place of gratitude to please God. I knew I needed to exercise faith and start confessing everything the Holy Spirit revealed to me as sin in my life. Romans 14:23 says that "whatever is not of faith is sin." This process of confession is amazing. When the Holy Spirit shows you things in your life that bring harm to you and others, they are contrary to how God desires you to live. This is when it's time to confess those things as sins. Remember, with our natural reasoning, we may not think certain behaviors will harm us or other people. If we give in to our human reasoning, we are not exercising faith. We are exercising our way of thinking that was programmed at some point in our life's journey.

Many times, the way we think was downloaded to us by our parents or other adults who influenced us. If their thinking wasn't led by God's gracious, unconditional love, then our thinking would just follow the same adopted pattern without even questioning it. We will assume it is right. Assumption welcomes pride. Pride never wants to look at another way. As the Scripture says, "There is a way that 'seems' right, but the end is death." This is how broken and unhealthy belief systems are created.

Confession is powerful and opens the door for humility to come in. Humbling ourselves before God by admitting we have sinned allows us to recognize His grace at work in the process. The Eternal Word says, "He gives grace to the humble" *(James 4:6)*. We're going to need His grace if we are going to get free.

Let me use myself as an example for confession. The Holy Spirit showed me that I was holding on to other forms of unforgiveness and bitterness from past betrayals in my life, so my confession went something like this:

"Holy Spirit, thank you for showing me that I am holding on to unforgiveness and bitterness in my heart. I don't want these things to control me any longer! I confess, by faith, that unforgiveness and bitterness are sins. I release them to You and ask You to take them from me as far as the east is from the west. Help me to forgive others who have hurt me, as You have forgiven me so graciously, in Jesus' name. Please replace the unforgiveness and bitterness with Your mercy and compassion."

This is just a snapshot, as there were so many things that needed to be confessed. I have written hundreds, perhaps thousands, of confessions over the years and seen how God has been faithful in delivering me from them all. I choose to remain open to this process as the Holy Spirit continues to highlight areas in me that He is wanting me to let go of. Do you get the idea? It's not a quick ten-minute session with the Holy Spirit. Whatever it is that God shows you by His Spirit, be faithful to confess it and release it to Him. Train yourself to sit quietly and listen to Him love on you as you go through this process. He will shower you with His goodness if you allow Him to.

I love imagery. It is a very powerful and effective tool to see myself disposing of the trash that doesn't benefit my soul. In my mind's eye, I then picture the Father who loves me, replacing the nasty things with His joy and peace. I picture how Jesus became every single one of the sins I'm confessing. *(2 Corinthians 5:21)* Wow. Unfathomable.

When we give it to Him, God is faithful to help us grow in His grace. His Spirit will continue to lead us and guide us into all truth. Keep asking Him to continue lighting your path as you begin to experience the weight of sin being lifted!

After confessing what He shows us is sin, there is something we can do next to increase our faith in the power of the cross. This brings us to the second "C."

CRUCIFY is the next step to getting free.

Most Christians would pretty much think of Jesus when they see the word crucify, as He in fact did die by crucifixion. It is a strong word, but it is intended to be a strong weapon against the enemy.

We find this very word used in the Book of Galatians to illustrate what a follower of Christ must do to grow in love:

"Those who belong to Christ have nailed their natural evil desires to his cross and crucified them there." Galatians 5:24 *(TLB)*.

Let's be clear on what warrants "natural evil desires" according to God. Remember, we may have our own understanding as to what natural evil desires are, but again, our perspectives are different from God's. He knows it all. We don't know what's best for us, even though pride will make us feel a false sense of being good.

In Chapter 5 of Galatians, we see a list of these natural desires God calls evil:

"But when you follow your own wrong inclinations, your lives will produce these evil results: impure thoughts, eagerness for lustful pleasure, idolatry, spiritism (that is, encouraging the activity of demons), hatred and fighting, jealousy and anger, constant effort to get the best for yourself, complaints and criticisms, the feeling that everyone else is wrong except those in your own little group—and there will be wrong doctrine, envy, murder, drunkenness, wild parties, and all that sort of thing…" Galatians 5:19-21 *(TLB)*.

You may recall many of these things listed are mentioned at the beginning of this book. They are found in unhealthy relationships that, in some cases, may have resulted in the pain of betrayal. Jesus came to deliver us from all that pain so we could be free to love as God intended us to, from the beginning. Now that is true freedom. To never be held back from loving and trusting again.

Only through the process will we see beneficial results.

When the Holy Spirit reveals the things holding you back from loving yourself and those in the world around you, He gives you a choice. Instead of making excuses or trying to justify your feelings, choose to confess these things as sin and picture yourself crucifying them to the cross, where Jesus paid the price for them. I'm not saying you are to deny your feelings. Acknowledge them before God and surrender them to Him. He can handle them far better than we ever could. So much of my life was controlled by my emotions in the past. It robbed me of His peace. Today, I'm happy to let the Holy Spirit guide my emotions. Great lesson learned.

I can't stress enough the importance of seeking God to reveal what it is we need to surrender. He cannot free us without our cooperation. Pride is the weapon formed against us that would prevent us from hearing God's voice. Pride won't prosper. No weapon formed against us will. But these weapons can certainly hinder us from an intimate walk with God.

Pride seems to work closely with deception. These, I believe, are the two deepest roots that will poison our identity in God. They influence our thoughts and emotions in many subtle ways, blinding us from seeing the truth about who we are and what our purpose is. We need the Holy Spirit's help if we are going to have our eyes opened. Crucifying pride and deception to the cross opens our eyes to see and ears to hear how Jesus died for those very things to set us free from their control. They must be annihilated from our hearts and minds so we can grow in God's grace and love.

I found that pride is something I often confess as a sin in my life, as well as crucifying it to the cross. The reason for this, I believe, is because there are so many forms that pride comes in. (More on this in Chapter 5.)

Think about how many beliefs you have from the time you were born. Most, if not all those beliefs came from a place of what others told us to believe. We were conditioned through experiences outside of God's presence. In other words, we were eating from "the tree of the knowledge of good and evil," making decisions about what we thought was right and wrong. Those thoughts started in our flesh nature and are found in the Scripture verses listed in Galatians 5:19-21. These are the very things we get to nail to the cross that Jesus Christ paid for, once and for all. He not only paid for them. He became them.

FREEDOM to LOVE well is the goal here.

The beautiful thing about Jesus is that He was willing to go through the process of rejection, betrayal, verbal, emotional, and physical abuse, torture, and abandonment so that you and I could be set free from all these things and more! He trusted God the Father throughout all the shameful acts of men who literally tore His flesh apart. Every one of His bones could be counted *(Psalm 22:17 NRSV)*. He knew that each one of us was on the other side of His suffering when He told the weeping women on His way to Calvary, "... Do not weep for me, but weep for yourselves and for your children" *(Luke 23:28 ESV)*. That would be us.

He made the way for us to break free by overcoming a world of suffering, a world stained by sin. This is real love. It's supernatural. To lay one's life down for another is a lifestyle of outgoing concern. It's esteeming others better than ourselves *(Philippians 2:3)*. This passage doesn't say everyone except for your betrayer/s or those who've hurt you. True love, the Bible says, "covers a multitude of sins" *(1 Peter 4:8 ESV)*. Now, let's be clear on what I am not saying here. To protect our hearts, we are not going to continue doing life with one who abuses or habitually betrays us. In fact, I would not have returned to my marriage if the Lord had instructed me not to. He had a merciful plan for my former husband and still does. He had to be the one to remove me from the relationship in His timing when it was clear that my former husband didn't want to change.

I think those of us who have experienced the mercy and forgiveness of God are thankful He didn't give up on us when we ignored His efforts to draw us to Himself. And even after seeing the truth, it may have taken multiple times for us before we let Him captivate our hearts and truly repented. He is so good. He is relentless in chasing us down. His love is so deep and wide toward us. Oh! The power of the cross!

Crucifying our sins to the cross is not crucifying our emotions. Emotions are a gift from our Creator and intend to be experienced as part of our being. What we do with our emotions and how we handle them could lead to sin. Give yourself permission to feel, even if you were told not to, at a younger age.

We must allow ourselves to feel the pain of betrayal, but then we must bring that pain to Jesus. He paid for it at the cross. We must trust that He will deal with the hurting person who hurt us. We have all done rotten things in life. It isn't our job to choose which things are worse or better than our own shortcomings. This would be eating from the tree of the knowledge of good and evil; choosing for ourselves who has the greater sin.

Jesus knew Judas would betray Him, and even after the kiss of His betrayer, He called him "friend" *(Matthew 26:48-50)*. Some commentators suggest that the term friend is better translated as "companion." The Greek word in this context is *"etaipos"* which means "Companion, friend, comrade" Even so, Jesus did not retaliate for the choice made by Judas, who walked with him for over three years. He chose to trust His Father's plan.

Now you may be saying to yourself as you read this, "But that's Jesus! I could never do what He did after someone betrayed me!" That's a valid feeling for sure. We can choose to stay locked up in that feeling, which will only lead to more hate, bitterness, rage, etc. … or we can surrender those negative feelings to the One who understands our pain. He endured that cross for our eternal benefit. We need to validate His selfless sacrifice over and above our feelings if we are going to experience His peace. It's not easy if we aren't willing to surrender our desire to retaliate. That is part of our human nature under the sway of the serpent. He opposes anything that would result in love, peace, and joy. He is the author of weapons formed against us humans. Don't let yourself be entertained by destructive thoughts. Those who dwell on destructive thoughts end up doing destructive things if they aren't released to God.

You are more than a conqueror through Christ who loves you!! *(Romans 8:37)*. Crucify your fleshly desires to the cross. Forever.

The third "C" and the next step in this process is CLEANSE.

What would happen if we were to go a year without showering? Ok, let's just say two weeks. There would be a bit of a stench, to say the least. Physically, we probably wouldn't be able to stand ourselves, let alone get around others. Thank the good Lord for soap and water!

When we speak of cleansing in the spirit realm, God has provided a way for us to stay spiritually clean from sin in our lives. Believe me, I'm sure there is such a thing as a stench in God's nostrils when it comes to sin. This is why the blood of His precious Son was poured out. It not only atoned for our sins but must also be utilized as a source of our continual cleansing. The cleansing process is ongoing as we are still living in a sinful world and are influenced by its ways.

The greater awareness we have of God in us, the quicker we will be able to confess our sins, crucify them to the cross, and cover them in the blood of Jesus, cleansing ourselves.

1 John 1:7 says this: "But if we walk in the light as He is in the light, we have fellowship with one another, and the blood of Jesus Christ His Son cleanses us from all sin" *(NKJV)*. Did you notice here that we must walk in the light as He is in the light? Light brings exposure. Things that may have happened to us years ago can be brought to light if we are willing to allow the Holy Spirit to show us the things that have been hidden. Hidden things are in the dark. We are deceived

into thinking they're not there. Even worse, self-deception will try to tell us that God doesn't see our "hidden" faults. Please know that He sees into every chamber of our hearts. Nothing is hidden from Him *(Hebrews 4:13)*.

Certain behaviors that are played out subconsciously are not always edifying. We wonder to ourselves, "Where did that come from?" We can't figure out what made us do it, so we head to a psychiatrist or local counselor for help in understanding. I'd like to suggest that you can be spared from spending your hard-earned money on specialists who will only be able to tap into that part of you that feels and reasons. Remember earlier we discussed that we are beings comprised of spirit, soul, and body?

Some educated specialists who have studied the human mind are wonderful when it comes to helping us see things with a fresh perspective or helping us identify feelings and sort them out. That is the knowledge that can help to some degree, but it won't deliver us. Only God can do that. On the other hand, a Holy Spirit-led, gifted counselor will be able to point us to the spiritual principles of the Kingdom of God. They will encourage us with the Holy Spirit's help to hear from the Lord for ourselves. We all need a close relationship with Jesus. So close that we will be able to talk and listen to Him about anything and everything—the good, the bad, and the ugly.

Deeper than our soul is our spirit. Ecclesiastes 11:5 says, "God's ways are as mysterious as the pathway of the wind and as the manner in which a human spirit is infused into the little body of a baby while it is yet in its mother's womb" *(TLB)*.

Our spirit is the part of us that can understand the things of God. It's the place where He set eternity in us *(Ecclesiastes 3:11)*. The inner man is your human spirit. When you start living for God and begin a relationship with Jesus Christ, your spirit is made aware of His presence in you. He begins to transform your behavior as you allow Him to renew your mind, which operates in the soul part of you.

The renewal process involves being cleansed first from our old way of thinking. This old way focuses on self-gratification. Before meeting Jesus, it's all about self. To be renewed in our thinking is to be God-minded, or another way of saying it is love-minded. To learn from the Holy Spirit how to shift our thinking, we will have to lay down what we think is right and listen to what He has to say.

Are we ready? Are we willing to obey what He shows us? This is what He requires of us to be transformed!

The blood of Jesus cleanses us of all unrighteousness as we confess our sins to Him *(1 John 1:9)*. So, it is imperative that we embrace the process if we want to be free from the effects of betrayal and all sin for that matter. Many professing Christians love God but are still miserable. I was one of them before committing myself to this process of cleansing. I would dare say that dying to our "old man" is a lot of work. It's hard to give up what's familiar to us.

Let the cleansing power of the Son of God's blood wash you regularly of all the soul and flesh clutter that builds up when left unchecked. Don't neglect your spiritual baths. Your love walk depends on it!

Last but not least of the four "C's" is CULTIVATE.

This last "C" that was revealed to me seems to be the one we will spend more time discussing since, originally, I had thought about the last "C" being "Closure." This writing project seemed to come to a halt for several months as I thought the book was pretty much finished. That is, until I asked the Lord why it was taking so many years to finish when I was certain He told me to write this book on *Betrayal*. It's amazing when we ask our Lord humbly the right questions. He is so ready to give us His answers. I can't believe I didn't think to ask Him before so much time went by. Ughh. It sure wasn't Him holding up this project. It was my lack of specifically asking if there was more, He wanted me to write or remove from what was already written. Wow. Do you know what He spoke to me in my heart when I sat quietly and waited?

He said, "I gave you the first 3 'C's, Teresa. You thought up the last one."

Whoa! I realized I was assuming that after doing the first three, there must be closure. I didn't wait on Him to continue with the last "C."

I learned a very valuable lesson about myself here. I realized how quickly we can jump into our flesh nature. Holy Spirit gave me His peace when I heard, "You can get right back into the Spirit, just as fast as you got into the flesh." I remembered I was not the one in charge of this delicate subject on the Father's heart. I repented, gave Him back the control to write what He wanted, and asked, "Father, what would you like the 4th 'C' to be?"

He said, "Your idea of 'Closure' suggests an ending. After the first 3 'C's, the real work begins. It is a deeper internal work. It is a continual process. It goes on for eternity. Therefore, it is not a closure by any means. **I want the last 'C' to be 'Cultivate.' My children will be cultivating pure hearts, holiness, pure minds, pure relationships, and pure INTIMACY with Me** after confessing, crucifying, and cleansing."

Our intimacy with the Lord will go on for eternity!!

God desires for each one of us to fulfill our destiny. That's why He has given us His Spirit to help us. He is our Helper, our Counselor, and our Comforter. If you have been betrayed, there is a good chance you picked up this book in hopes of finding some answers to some hard-core questions.

Why such cruelty exists in our world is to know that there is an evil spiritual force at work to steal, kill, and destroy all that represents God. As mentioned earlier, Satan is the adversary of God. He hates human beings because we are made in the very image of God. He hates us because he knows that we are going to judge the angels *(1 Corinthians 6:3)*. He ultimately hates God. If we have hatred in our hearts toward one another, we now know who it comes from. It is not of God.

God does hate things but not people. He hates sin, evil, and everything else that would take His children away from Him, His love, and His abundant life. The enemy knows that we will rejoice and prosper in life when love is our reason for living.

Hating people will only destroy us, as it has in so many relationships, throughout history.

Hatred was birthed, not in the Garden of Eden, but it all started in Heaven when love was replaced with jealousy, envy, and pride in Lucifer's heart.

Pride is the root that corrupted Lucifer's character *(Ezekiel 28:17)*, turning him against his Maker. It is in the works of the flesh you will see those same traits operating. Those evil traits are the things that block us from receiving God's love and purpose for our lives. They keep us from cultivating a pure heart—a heart that was designed to have intimacy with its Maker.

When we tear down obstacles found namely in the "old self," and begin to operate in who God says we are, we will be free to cultivate a heart filled with His love. We will be growing in His character. We will ultimately come into the full knowledge of who we are in Christ. Truly, we will live and move and have our being in God. Holy Spirit will help us through God's living and active Word, and through a community of other believers. We can't do it on our own. It is important to ask God to lead you to a community of believers that are humbly seeking His presence and walking in His Kingdom principles, reaching out to the poor and destitute. You will find healing and restoration in that type of environment, where you will then be a vessel of love to help others.

Praise the living Christ! God's Kingdom Plan is continuing to unfold on the earth! Many sons and daughters are becoming more aware that they are carriers of His presence! Christ in us is the hope of Glory! Jesus Himself said the Kingdom of God is within us!! *(Luke 17:21 NKJV)*.

Jesus has given us as believers the authority to trample on serpents and scorpions and over ALL the power of the enemy! *(Luke 10:19)*. We can take authority over betrayal and its effects on our souls. We must demonstrate our faith in these words of Jesus, to experience a new life in Him!

Christ Himself made the way for us. Thank you, Jesus.

Betrayal is a weapon formed against humanity to sever us from relationships with each other and especially with our Heavenly Father. No wonder Jesus reversed the effects of it by willingly allowing the kiss of the enemy through one of His companions. He took that betrayal kiss to the cross with Him to show us that He would love through the act of forgiveness.

When we follow Christ's example by forgiving those who hurt us, we are freeing ourselves from the clutches of betrayal. When we express love through forgiveness as Jesus did, we are crushing the enemy's head. We are destroying his evil work in our lives and reminding him that the love in us is the greater force. We will begin to experience a peace that transcends our finite reasoning. God's peace will usher in the freedom to receive more of His mercy and grace for others when we realize how forgiven we are!

Back to the critical importance of the fourth "C." Cultivate. How do we cultivate a heart like Jesus? How important is it to God, who desires our hearts to be intimate with Him?

True intimacy is when two become one of like mind. It's when two hearts beat as one and understand each other deeply. Jesus prayed to the Father in John 17 that we would become one with Him, as He and the Father are one. How interested are we in answering Jesus's prayer? He always prayed with the Father's heart. We are called to be the answer to that prayer by becoming one with Jesus.

When we choose to obey the Word, we cultivate mindsets agreeing with Him. His words reflect His heart. The more we agree with His words (His thinking), the more we will be reflecting His heart. It takes more than just reading what Jesus thinks in the Bible. We must ACTIVATE His words BY DOING them. ACTIVATE to CULTIVATE. This is called, "putting feet to our faith." By declaring, decreeing, and living out the Word of God, we are ABSOLUTELY cultivating His heart and lifestyle of holiness. It is impossible to develop a LOVE lifestyle without being IN love with Him. We must do as Jesus did. PRAY. A prayer life is critical to becoming all God has called us to be in Christ. Prayer is sitting with God. Making space on a daily, continual basis for a two-way conversation. Just as you would sit with anyone at a table, sharing what's on each other's minds. He will speak to you and share His thoughts as you read His Written Word. Sitting quietly after asking Him questions, will allow you to hear His beautiful voice. You will know love is talking with you. It's the ONLY way to build a relationship with Him.

WE MUST PRACTICE HIS PRESENCE.

When we choose the love walk, we will begin cultivating a pure heart.

"Blessed are the pure in heart for they will see God" *(Matthew 5:8 NIV)*.

Ephesians 5:2 tells us to walk in love. We are to be imitators of Christ Jesus. This is a sweet-smelling aroma to God. Walking in love is to abide in God. It's how we cultivate a deep relationship with Him. It's one choice at a time. Do we live for Him? Or do we live for ourselves?

He makes it clear in John 15:4-10: "Abide in Me, and I in you. As the branch cannot bear fruit of itself, unless it abides in the vine, neither can you, unless you abide in Me. I am the vine; you are the branches. He who abides in Me, and I in him, bears much fruit; for without Me you can do nothing. If anyone does not abide in Me, he is cast out as a branch and is withered; and they gather them and throw them into the fire, and they are burned. If you abide in Me, and My words abide in you, you will ask what you desire, and it shall be done for you. By this My Father is glorified, that you bear much fruit; so you will be My disciples. As the Father loved Me, I also have loved you; abide in My love.If you keep My commandments, you will abide in My love, just as I have kept My Father's commandments and abide in His love" *(NKJV)*.

There is so much in these seven verses. The New King James Version uses the word "Abide" ten times. Jesus is creating a picture of what a believer's relationship with Him should look like. He tells us that our lives will bear much fruit if we stay attached to Him. *Meinate (Strong's 3306 [e] Biblehub.com)* is the English font of the Greek word for "Abide" here in John 15. We would not be able to abide in Christ without His Spirit abiding in us. We must never sever ourselves from the vine, or we [our true selves, our individual purpose] will dry up and die spiritually.

In other words, we will be devoted wholeheartedly, without reservation, to Christ and Christ alone. We will partner with Him in everything, relying on His Spirit in us and not our own efforts. He will be our number one. Out of our relationship will flow living water, peace like a river. Anything OUTSIDE of this relationship leads to self-deception. Self-deception distorts a believer's perception of their relationship with the Father, Jesus, and Holy Spirit. This condition called "self-deception" can go so far as to convince a believer that their lifestyle is "still okay," if they just "check in" with God now and then. The believer will still confess they are a Christian because they prayed a certain prayer years before. They may have gotten water baptized and even received the Baptism of The Holy Spirit. Many go through these motions *but never surrender the way they think, feel, or choose in their everyday life.* Subconsciously, they have put all these things on a shelf, feeling secure in their spiritual experience at the time. Self-deception is ugly. This is why many of these unsuspecting "Christians" can't understand why, after doing these things, they are still depressed, some suicidal, and just discouraged most of the time. They are led to feel forgotten by God. So, they never make any effort to develop a deep relationship with Him. This is totally a ploy of the enemy. God will not give up on us.

What I have just described here is called a "CINO," Christians In Name Only *(Urban Dictionary.com)*. They may have the right "Christianese verbiage" when speaking with others, but their actions consistently contradict their words. Let's look at Matthew 15:8-9: "Isaiah was right when he prophesied about you; 'These people honor Me with their lips, but their hearts are far from Me. They worship Me in vain; their teachings are merely human rules'" *(NIV)*. These are professing Christians who are led by the world's standards, their carnal nature, and influenced by whatever looks good at the time. Their false identities are continuing to rule their hearts rather than allowing the Holy Spirit to restore their identity in Christ.

I'm not referring to those who still make mistakes and fall but are humble, heartfelt followers of Jesus, who are positioning themselves at His feet in a truly repentant place. I'm not talking about those who recognize they desperately, constantly need the Lord's help to live and move and have their being in Him. There will be growth in every true Christian that does this.

A believer who is gifted to retain the words in the Bible and to share them eloquently is not how God defines those who are His. He defines HIMSELF in His beloved children. His DNA can be summed up in a four-letter word: L-O-V-E.

He has placed beautiful expressions of Himself in each one of us. They were given from the foundation of the world to be expressed throughout eternity, to bring Him glory. Many use God's gifts to bring glory to themselves. The flesh nature ALWAYS wants to steal the glory away from God. The flesh nature *(aka carnal nature)* is the "old man" the Bible talks about. It's that way of thinking that takes us down a familiar path, leading to destruction. God desires for us to live full lives with our contentment in Him. He is the Way, the Truth, and the LIFE. He doesn't want any of His children to be destroyed by taking the wrong path. If we call ourselves a Christ-follower, then we must choose daily to say "yes" to Him as He leads us in His way! Matthew 16:24-25 makes it clear, directly from the heart of Jesus: "If anyone desires to come after Me, let him deny himself, and take up his cross, and follow Me" *(NKJV)*.

The more we say "no" to Him, the more we begin to slip into deception, thus becoming a CINO.

To me, one of the most terrifying Scriptures in all the Bible is:

"On that day many will say to Me, 'Lord, Lord, did we not prophesy in Your name, and cast out demons in your name, and do many mighty works in Your name?' And then will I declare to them, 'I never knew you; depart from me, you workers of lawlessness'" *(Matthew 7:22-23 ESV)*. Jesus says, "many" will say these things to Him, believing they could just perform good deeds without a deep love in their hearts for Him. Are we using His holy name for our personal gain? We are to seek Him and love Him more than the works He does through us. We must guard our hearts. God will not share His glory with anyone. *(Isaiah 42:8 NCV)*

Deception will lead us to believe God is pleased with us by deeds alone, performed in His name. He looks at the heart. He always has and always will. The heart is where deception hides and must be cleansed by the One who formed it, or we are with no hope at all *(Jeremiah 17:9)*. Jesus came to bring us ETERNAL HOPE in Him. For Him to do that, He had to come to the earth and live among us humans to demonstrate what a pure, undefiled heart looks like by the way He lived in a world corrupted by sin.

Satan is after our soul. When we think, feel, and choose, we MUST surrender every one of our thoughts, feelings, and choices to the God of the Universe. If we don't, we open ourselves up to the enemy of our souls. This is why it is SO IMPORTANT to abide in Christ. He is the lover and protector of our souls if we let Him be.

As a Christian, for years I struggled with how to live an abundant life that God promises to give all those who follow Him. I would read passages such as Isaiah 44:3:

"For I will give you abundant water for your thirst and for your parched fields. And I will pour out My Spirit and My blessings on your children" *(TLB)*.

Over time, as I continued my journey with the Lord, I realized these promises could be deeply embraced with a heart cultivated in unconditional love. Notice, I said over time. Relationships are built over time. The more time we spend and invest in a relationship, the more intimate it will become. The secret is to abide in Jesus. I like to think of Jesus as the "love language" of God.

God shows us in His Word how our relationship with Him begins:

The first step is to confess with our mouths and believe in our hearts that Jesus is Lord, and that God raised Him from the dead *(Romans 10:9)*. That means He is given our permission to enter our personal world with all the good, bad, and uglies. It's when we come to grasp that our way hasn't worked. We find ourselves yearning for peace and happiness in our lives.

A powerful restoration awaits all those who accept the truth that Jesus, the Son of God, Son of Man, redeemed them from the curse of the law of sin and death.

We must choose to believe that He loves us like no human ever could. We must allow the Holy Spirit to convince us that God is our source of inner healing. We must personally acknowledge that without His grace, we are helpless and hopeless.

Gratitude should rise inside all those who discover that Jesus wiped out the root of sin by becoming sin itself. 2 Corinthians 5:21 says, "God made him who had no sin to be sin for us, so that in him we might become the righteousness of God" *(NIV)*. Jesus is the One who brought GRACE and TRUTH to the earth so that we could turn from our spiritual diets of eating from the fruit of the tree of the knowledge of good and evil (self-centered desires) and turn toward Him. His Word is our eternal sustenance. Jesus Christ is the vine. He is the Tree of LIFE. We must be connected [branches] to produce His abundant fruit in this life and for all eternity. He sustains us as we "press toward the goal for the prize of the upward call of God in Christ Jesus" *(Philippians 3:14 NKJV)*.

Jesus modeled what surrender looks like. Hebrews 5:8 says that Jesus learned obedience by the things which He suffered. This is humility in action. That kind of humility brought *grace and truth* to each of us as an example of how to live. There was no pride in Jesus.

On the other hand, every human being has sinned and fallen short of God's glory. Not one is righteous. Pride is part of the sin package we've all inherited at birth. This is why, through Jesus, we must be born again—of the Spirit. Once born again, we are not exempt from pain and suffering. If Jesus suffered (and boy, did he!), we will also share in His sufferings.

The Apostle Paul explains the Christian life best in his writing to the Church at Philippi. Here it is in the Amplified Version: "And this, so that I may know Him [experientially, becoming more thoroughly acquainted with Him, understanding the remarkable wonders of His Person more completely] and [in that same way experience] the power of His resurrection [which overflows and is active in believers], and [that I may share] the fellowship of His sufferings, by being continually conformed [inwardly into His likeness even] to His death [dying as He did]; so that I may attain to the resurrection [that will raise me] from the dead" *(Philippians 3:10-11).*

Looking at these Scriptures, we can see how part of the process of getting to know Jesus in a deeper way, we must share in His sufferings. This doesn't mean we are to physically succumb to the works of darkness in our lives. It means we are to humble ourselves by dying to those things we are comfortable with doing, outside of God's boundaries of love. It isn't easy to surrender to His way of obedience. Our flesh nature is 100 percent opposed to it! The flesh suffers when it must bow to the righteousness of Jesus.

It is a courageous act to let go of pride and cling to humility. Humility is the key to our Heavenly Father's heart. It releases His grace into our lives. This is the heart being cultivated in you as you confess your sins, crucify them to the cross, and cleanse them in the blood of Jesus. This process allows our faith in God to grow.

Get ready to receive His unlimited grace!!

By allowing God to dig deep and cultivate the soil of our hearts, we can be filled with refreshing rivers of living water from Him. We can bloom in the light of His presence. We can flourish in every season of life. We can experience a truly abundant life on earth as it is in heaven.

What a wonderful, abundant life it is to walk in freedom from the lies we were living before meeting our Redeemer!! As we are miraculously transformed from the inside, we can be assured that it is God who works in us to will and to act to fulfill His good purpose *(Philippians 2:13)*. He also promises to complete the work that He began in us *(Philippians 1:6)*.

Did you know that God has an eternal goal for you? It's found in Colossians 2:2:

"My goal is that they may be encouraged in heart and united in love, so that they may have the full riches of complete understanding, in order that they may know the mystery of God, namely Christ" *(NIV)*.

So, my friend, don't be surprised if the devil hits you with discouragement and division against another human. He works his armies against the goals of God, but he will never win when we take hold of God's love and take the enemy's kiss of betrayal to Jesus Christ, who defeated our foes. Satan shudders to think that we can have the full riches of complete understanding to know Christ.

The devil is the author of confusion and the father of lies. When we turn to the Word of God, which is Truth *(John 17:17)*, he has no defense because his exposure comes through the Word of God. No one knows the enemy's tactics better than God. His Word will rightly divide the truth we struggle with between our injured souls and our spirit that connects with God. Without His Word, we are left to our wretched voices of the past. Look here:

"The Word of God is living and active. It is sharper than any sword that has two edges. It cuts deep enough to separate soul from spirit ... it judges the thoughts and purposes of the heart" *(Hebrews 4:12 NIRV)*.

Thank God Jesus came as our Way to Grace, Truth, and Freedom.

One last thing I want to mention here is that when we forgive others, it is God's strategy of love so that we can be made whole and immersed in His peace. It's not to say we are to associate with or condone the behavior of those who have pierced our hearts, emotionally wounding us. They will have to answer to God for themselves. As believers, we are to obey what God's Word tells us to do. He tells us to "put on tender mercies, kindness, humility, meekness, longsuffering; bearing with one another, and forgiving one another, if anyone has a complaint against another, even as Christ forgave you, **so you also must do**" (The emphasis is mine), *(Colossians 3:12, 13 NKJV)*.

True forgiveness forgets, permanently letting go. Humanly, this is impossible. But IN CHRIST, ALL things are possible. Psalm 103:12 tells us that God has removed our transgressions from us, as far as the East is from the West. In another Scripture, Hebrews 8:12, God declares, "I will forgive their wickedness and will remember their sins no more." Before encountering Jesus, we were among over 8 billion humans who were committing adultery, spiritually, against our Maker. We were doing life without Him and idolizing people and things. We were unfaithful to our God in heaven.

So how are we to treat those who have done us dirty? We are not more righteous than God. With His help, we must surrender those wrongdoings toward us to the One who shows us that we must forgive and forget another's sin against us. We sinned against our Loving Creator as a lifestyle, before coming to know Him, and He continually forgives us. We owe Him a debt we cannot pay. So, what does He do? He washes all our sin debt away in His Son's shed blood.

To be relieved of such debt and not pay it forward is to be like the wicked servant in the parable found in Matthew 18:23-35. The Master had canceled all his debt, yet the forgiven servant refused to do the same when someone else needed forgiveness of a much smaller debt. It is non-productive to hold onto unforgiveness. It cripples us from growing in the grace and knowledge of our Lord and Savior, Jesus Christ. When we can let go of someone else's sin against us, we are beginning to cultivate a heart after God's own.

How do we know if we have truly been set free from unforgiveness? When we can honestly lift them up to our Lord in prayer with heartfelt compassion, no longer experiencing the negative, painful emotions associated with the event, we have been healed. We are becoming more like Jesus. Obviously, to do this is a witness that Christ indeed is living richly on the inside of us! Of and by ourselves this is impossible, but as mentioned earlier, with God all things are possible!

PRAYER IS THE PROCESS OF CULTIVATING THE SOIL OF OUR HEARTS.

Without talking and listening to God, without building a relationship with Him, we will be unable to fully experience True Freedom in Christ. Prayer is the most important aspect of our Christian Walk. Without prayer, it's like trying to unlock a deadbolt without the key. It will remain locked. Prayer is the key to unlocking the deadbolts in the areas of our souls that have been hidden and kept in bondage. God has always known what is in there. We can call on Him to open our locked-up hearts. He is gentle and will not force us to give Him anything we are not ready to surrender. The important thing is to engage with God in conversation. Be honest with Him. He's a better listener than any human. Ask Him to help you listen for His direction and counsel.

In cultivating a prayer life, you can't help but get free. In His presence is where you will find everything you need. Sitting quietly is not a common practice of our day, so it may feel awkward at first. I encourage you to resist the temptation to keep busy. The enemy does not want us to sit quietly and listen to God's loving words toward us. To break through, you must do a new thing. The devil is a liar. You can hear from God.

Let us work together with the Master of our hearts to cultivate an intimate relationship with Him in all things. Intimacy with Jesus will keep us from the wiles of the enemy.

Intimacy with Jesus will lead to holiness. Holy is what He calls us to be, as He is. To be holy, we must hate what He hates. The Lord hates sin, pride, and every form of evil. To fear the Lord is to hate evil *(Proverbs 8:13)*.

Let's explore a little bit about pride.

CHAPTER FIVE
UNVEILING PRIDE

Never underestimate the power of pride. It comes in various forms and wears many masks. It is given power through deception. When we open our mind to sources outside the Word of God, we are risking our future of hope along with God's very best for us. I realize everyone who reads these words may choose not to believe them. That's the prerogative of free will, indeed.

We can choose not to believe that gravity exists as well. Laws exist whether we believe they do or not. This may be hard to swallow. What makes it so hard is the pride hiding behind what we believe. Only the Holy Spirit can lead us into all truth. In the Spirit, we find true life and its meaning. It is our job to humble ourselves and allow the Spirit of God to teach us if we truly want to understand life and love in relation to it.

When I allow the Holy Spirit to teach me, I like to picture the Bible as a holy filter that knowledge must pass through to get God's understanding.

Self-deception is likely one of our greatest blind spots. It is another "weapon formed against us." *(Isaiah 54:17)* Why? Because this is when we have convinced ourselves that we are right, and our hearts have become hardened (no longer open to another perspective) in that area of belief without filtering it through God's Word. Remember, God's Word is Truth *(John 17:17)*, whereas Jeremiah 17:9 says, "The heart is deceitful and desperately wicked …"

All of us are susceptible to becoming prideful. Especially if we don't have the powerful revelation of who we are in Christ. How do we view ourselves in relation to the world around us? Do we know we are just passing through? Do we realize there is a far greater world ahead of us? Is Jesus Christ in your eternity? In whom or what do you place your identity? Let's explore the following Scripture:

1 John 2:16: "For all that is in the world, the lust of the flesh, and the lust of the eyes, and the pride of life, is not of the Father, but is of the world" *(KJV)*.

If we place our identity in feelings, (lust of the flesh), material things (lust of the eyes), or our own or others' accomplishments (pride of life), we are deceived and living out a false identity. Sounds harsh if we were to take offense when reading these words. The truth is, when we place our identity in these things, we are relying on ourselves as well as the things of this world, and there is a galactic difference between the spirit of the world and the Spirit of God. Please don't misunderstand what is being said here. We are to be in the world but not of the world. What does this mean? God placed us here and desires for us to prosper in every way! Jesus would not have come to this earth if God didn't want us to experience abundant life *(John 10:10)*. Where the issue arises is how we humans perceive what the abundant life means. What does it look like to you? If Christ came so that we could have an abundant life, then that would mean He holds the keys to understanding this kind of living.

In other words, without Jesus, we cannot have an abundant life filled with love, joy, peace, patience, kindness, goodness, faithfulness, gentleness, and self-control. Why? Because Jesus Christ is all these things and desires for us to be set free from the stress and worries of everyday living in this world.

Like the serpent in the garden, the world continuously offers a seemingly better way for us to achieve health, wealth, status, and happiness through its own means apart from a real and loving God. The same goes for how we relate to one another. When we aren't content with who we are, we will find ourselves trying to create an identity that somehow makes us feel accepted and loved. As was mentioned earlier in this book, the deepest need within human hearts is to love and be loved.

The difference between a false identity and a true identity, is that one relies on others and/or circumstances to FEEL loved and accepted. The other relies on God and KNOWS they are loved and accepted. Our identity is all about God in us. Without truth, we are deceived, and when we are deceived, pride rules our hearts. We can live in this world knowing who we are in Christ. When we walk in His ways, we will be of Him and not of the world.

Regarding Christ, Psalm 25:9 says, "He guides the humble in what is right and teaches them his way" *(NIV)*.

Humility is the key to unveiling pride. Jesus invites us to come to Him to find rest for our souls. He will teach us the abundant life we have in Him. He will reveal to us who we really are and what a fulfilling destiny we all have. He alone can free us from every form of pride.

Matthew 11:29 says, "Take my yoke upon you. Let me teach you, because I am humble and gentle at heart, and you will find rest for your souls" *(NLT)*.

I want that kind of rest for my soul. To be stripped of pride allows our hearts to be open to learning the most excellent way of life, and that is one of love.

If, at this point, you are feeling agitated reading about pride, denying to yourself that you have any, humility is knocking at the door of your heart, ready to conquer those thoughts.

We will know we are not walking in pride when we are giving God all the credit for anything we have accomplished in life. Our gifts, talents, and abilities must all be expressed out of our true love for the Creator who built all that beauty inside of us. We do have our part in achieving goals, but the Lord is the One who gives us the desires and energy to achieve them. In this way, we know inside that He is receiving all the glory. Remember the vine and the branches? He is the vine. We are the branches. We MUST be connected for our lives to flourish with Kingdom meaning.

So, when we even say we are so proud of our children or loved ones, we must be careful that it is coming from a heart of gratitude toward God. With this heart, we are walking in humility.

We actually have nothing to do with what God placed on the inside of others, including our children. They are from Him. He placed abilities and gifts inside each one. As parents, we can encourage them to grow in their gifts as the Lord shows us what those gifts are. We can be excited and celebrate with them. We can be pleased with what the Lord has helped someone achieve in their lives. We can speak life to those things and pray for success in another person's walk.

There is a form of pride that likes to take the credit for someone else's accomplishments.

Also, as parents, it is important to validate and bring value to our children and those around us. It is a wise thing to check our hearts as to why we would take any credit for God's goodness and mercy in their lives.

Sadly, many parents are prideful over their children, deceitfully unaware they are attempting to live their own lives through their children. They base their own identity and value their loved ones, dependent on how productive their loved ones are in life. This takes the attention off God, who is the source behind whatever it took to bring that loved one to where they are.

Pride of self is ruling when God is out of the equation.

Society has conditioned us to be proud of just about everything. Proud of the baseball team that beat their opponent. Proud of the nation God birthed us into. In my case, I would be saying, "I'm proud to be an American" (like I chose my nation). Proud of someone's baking skills. Proud of the mayor. Proud of the neighbor potty training their dog not to make deposits on our property. (Haha. I know. This is a bit ridiculous, but it makes the point.) The list goes on and on.

Just using the word "proud" is done so loosely, without giving it any thought these days. I would just caution us to look at how it was integrated into our thinking. Human nature will try to justify everything. Ask the Holy Spirit to reveal why we speak it so much. Again, our belief system is what the serpent is after. Why do we believe it's okay to be proud of anything?

To be honest, most of the usage of the word has a wrong heart motive behind it. A reason for being proud is created in the thoughts. The reasoning may go something like this: "Because of what I've done ..." "Because of my skills ..." Because of my help, input, etc. ..." We've all thought these things more than we care to admit. I hate to say it, but this reflects selfish reasoning and builds a false identity through someone else's success or accomplishments—even our own. It makes us feel good to say we're proud. It may also be feeding pride to the recipient of our statement. All of this is happening on the subconscious level. We aren't even aware of it most of the time. It is very subtle.

To clarify, I am not speaking to those with a pure heart who see God in their loved one's accomplishments. God is getting the glory in those instances. Unfortunately, most are not thinking of God when they talk about being proud of others.

It is about the heart. Proverbs 16:5 *(NIV)* says, "The Lord detests all the proud of heart." We just need to check in with Him whenever we are about to express pride in ourselves and others. We must be careful to give God the glory.

Overcoming the root of pride is warfare between a person's soul, flesh nature, and their born-again spirit. Remember, our mind, will, emotions, and passions contain a flawed belief system. Our spirit, the deepest part of our being, is what connects us to God.

God's Spirit of Truth is trying to line up our souls with His Word. When we choose to agree with and do what His Word says, we are surrendering to the mind of Christ within us.

The world sees pride as good in many things.

In 1 John 2:15-17, it is written, "Do not love the world, or the things of the world. If anyone loves the world, the love of the Father is not in him. For all that is in the world—the lust of the flesh, the lust of the eyes, and **the pride of life**—is not of the Father but is of the world. And the world is passing away, and the lust of it; but he who does the will of God abides forever" *(NKJV)*.

It seems the world has conditioned us to take pride in our efforts, abilities, talents, accomplishments, etc. ...

We extend that pride into the lives of our loved ones without even realizing where it originated. It's not any fault of our own. Everyone does it, so we think it is normal to express pride in ourselves and others. Just a reminder that the tree of the knowledge of good and evil began the idea of choosing for ourselves what we believe is good and okay, and what is wrong and evil.

Please know my heart here. There is absolutely no condemnation for those who are in Christ Jesus. But before we were in Christ Jesus, we were trained to look at pride in a positive light in some ways. The Lord doesn't condemn. He opens our eyes to see the way He sees. His Spirit leads us and guides us into all truth. Pride is of the world. The world and all its ways are contrary to Heaven's ways. God gets all the glory. He doesn't share it with anyone.

The whole purpose of writing this chapter is to create an awareness of the Father's heart regarding this subject of pride. He is the only One that can take pride in His creation, as He is the Creator of all. But even so, in the book of Genesis, He says all that He created was good. He didn't say He was proud of all His work. Love created us. There is no pride in love *(1 Corinthians 13:1)*. God did say that He was "well pleased" with His Son, in Matthew 3:17. Let's investigate Thayer's Greek Lexicon to see what God meant when He inspired the writer to use these words.

The Greek word here, *eudokeo* pronounced "yoo-dok-eh'-o," means to think well of, approve (an act); especially to approbate (a person or thing): —think good. Be well pleased *(www.bibletools.org > eudokeo)*. When God says He is well pleased with us or our loved ones, He is expressing His heart and delight in us. In following God's example, we can be pleased and take delight in our accomplishments and others' accomplishments if we acknowledge in our hearts that it's because of His great work placed on the inside of us. All our gifts, talents, and abilities come from the Lord who made us. He deserves all the credit [glory]. Again, it is all about our heart behind the accolades. Remember when we praise others made in the image of God, we are to give God the highest praise for our achievements. Some true Olympians recognize this and have even publicly given God the credit for their gold medal achievements. Yes, humans do the work, but the Lord is the One who gives us the stamina and strength and health to achieve goals in life.

Our humble prayers and trust in God can help us to work hard and achieve much in our everyday lives. Prayers for our children and grandchildren, parents and siblings, friends and relatives are answered when we see them succeed in their life's journey. They may even be receiving awards and trophies. When they walk across a stage and receive a diploma; when we, or they, are recognized for outstanding accomplishments in life. If these things are done without prayer, that leaves us to take all the credit without God's help. In other words, this is an example of the "pride of life." The pride of life is something we are told is not from the Father but is from the world *(1 John 2:15-16 ESV)*. Let's look at yet another illustration here:

Some roots go very deep. There is a tree called "Shepherd's Tree," which is native to the Kalahari Desert. The depth of its roots was documented at 230 feet deep. *(rutgers.edu/news/deep-roots-plants-driven-soil-hydrology)*. I wonder how deep, spiritually speaking, the root of pride has dug its way into humanity since the Garden of Eden. Picture that, 230 feet deep. Yet pride in the human heart took root thousands of years ago. Generations have become so familiar with it that a sense of normalcy and acceptance of it has been part of humanity's culture.

Only the Holy Spirit can tear out the root of pride in a human heart when that heart is surrendered to Him.

This may be very controversial to many. Suppose there is no root of pride in us regarding this discussion. In that case, we shouldn't get offended at the possibility that pride itself may very well have betrayed us into thinking it's okay to be proud in certain areas or circumstances. Pride is subtle here. It's not the obvious form of seeing someone with an arrogant attitude. The serpent was also subtle. Pride, deception, and lies originated with him. These are all weapons formed against us.

Since we've already determined the author of pride, it would be wise to ask the Holy Spirit to show us the truth about weapons He has made available for us to overcome and win our battles. I want to be on the winning side, and Satan is NOT IT!

Holy Spirit, please, would you reveal more to us regarding this subject of pride? Open our eyes to understand how we can be pure in all our motives. Jesus, we trust that Your shed blood cleanses us from every form of pride as we confess it as sin. We love You for this and for everything that frees us from the clutches of this world's influence.

CHAPTER SIX
WEAPONS THAT PROSPER!

When God says, "No weapon formed AGAINST us will prosper," He means it.

That statement caused me to ponder on the possibility that there are weapons formed FOR us that will prosper! God wants you to be encouraged in knowing that He is always on your side. Let's look at what He has to say about His weapons that are intended to bring mass destruction to the darkness:

Ephesians 6:10-12 in the Message translation reads, "… God is strong, and He wants you strong. So, take everything the Master has set out for you, well-made weapons of the best materials. And put them to use so you will be able to stand up to everything the devil throws your way. This is no weekend war that we'll walk away from and forget about in a couple of hours. This is for keeps, a life-or-death fight to the finish against the devil and all his angels."

Let's continue in Ephesians 6:13-18: "Be prepared. You're up against far more than you can handle on your own. Take all the help you can get, every weapon God has issued, so that when it's all over but the shouting, you'll still be on your feet. Truth, righteousness and peace, faith, and salvation are more than words. Learn how to apply them. You'll need them throughout your life. God's Word is an indispensable weapon. In the same way, prayer is essential in this ongoing warfare. Pray hard and long. Pray for your brothers and sisters. Keep your eyes open. Keep each other's spirits up so that no one falls behind or drops out" *(The Message)*.

There is a wealth of information and instruction from God in these Scriptures. He wants to help us succeed in life. Success is overcoming anything that would hold us back from becoming who we were created to be.

Love must be the foundation of who we are. This is what God intended from the beginning. We have been given the free choice to return to *love's way*. Since prayer is an essential part of this process, it behooves us to discipline our minds, our wills, and our emotions to pray. In our spirit, we are willing to do this, but as the Bible states, our flesh is weak. It opposes the things of the Spirit, so we must press on!

The greatest thing we can do is to grow intimate with God. Through that intimacy, we will be able to effectively utilize the gifts of the Spirit, according to God's Word. Put another way, the sword of the Spirit, [the Word of God], is a powerful weapon when wielded in humility under love's direction.

1 Corinthians 14:1-2 says to "follow the way of love and eagerly desire gifts of the Spirit, especially prophecy. For anyone who speaks in a tongue does not speak to people but to God. Indeed, no one understands them; they utter mysteries by the Spirit" *(NIV)*.

Did you catch that? No one understands when someone speaks in a tongue but God. That means not even the devil understands the mysteries uttered by God's Spirit. Only by His Spirit can tongues be interpreted as well (another gift).

I've heard many Christians talk against this precious gift of the Spirit. Here's a thought: Why would this not be of God when the Bible says only God understands it? The devil has no defense against something he doesn't know is being prayed. So, it is no surprise that he would bombard us with thoughts of unbelief regarding this powerful weapon against him. It is a weapon FOR us to use, as believers. John the Baptist proclaimed that Jesus baptizes us in the Holy Spirit (Mark 1:8). In Matthew and Luke's accounts, it was written that Jesus would baptize with the Holy Spirit and fire *(Matthew 3:11; Luke 3:16 ESV)*.

Like anything in our Christian Walk, it takes faith to do what God tells us to do. When He says to pray in an unknown tongue, He knows it is going to benefit us. He is a good God. He is not out to trick us. Faith is what pleases Him. His ways are above our ways. I enjoy the fact that the enemy can't get an upper hand on my life when he hasn't got a clue as to what I'm talking to God about in a heavenly language. It's a win in the Spirit!

There is so much to be said on this subject that multiple volumes of books could be written. There are many books out there on the Baptism of the Holy Spirit, with evidence of speaking in tongues.

Whenever our minds go to a place of resistance, when we are presented with Scriptures that don't make sense to us, it is a hint that there may be hidden pride in our understanding. That is the time we humble ourselves and ask questions. Then wait. The Lord is not intimidated by our questions. He knows we struggle with our mind renewal. He is faithful to help us see with His eyes as we seek Him. If we don't do that, it could very well prevent us from receiving what the Lord has to say. We cannot receive the things of God in our hearts without faith in Him.

This weapon is what helped me break FREE from many years of accumulated soul wounds. I was baptized in the Holy Spirit at the time I repented and received Christ into my life back in 1982. I was praying in an unknown tongue after I was led in a prayer being told that Jesus is the One who baptizes in the Spirit. It's a gift received through faith in Him, just as my salvation was received. After that experience, I started to attend a non-Catholic church for the first time. Nothing was taught on this subject of baptism in the Holy Spirit, so I thought it was just a one-time experience. I put it on a shelf until many years later, when I started asking God about this again. I was led to a Pentecostal church when I heard others praying in tongues. This community seemed hungry for the things of God, but a little after a year of attending, the pastor admitted to the congregation that he had been having an affair with the youth leader. I knew this leadership obviously had some serious issues to deal with and was at peace leaving that toxicity behind. (I left sorrowfully, praying for this pastor's restoration, but especially for the precious congregation/sheep who were left in confusion after the announcement was made.) I noted to myself that all that praying in tongues does nothing, if our heart is not humble before God. Pride can even creep into that gift if we allow it to.

The next part of my journey... Remember, NEVER STOP asking, seeking, and knocking for the Lord's will, plan, and timing in your life. It is a discipline I try never to take for granted. The Throne Room of Grace is always available. Without God, I learned that I would just be returning to the wrong tree in the Garden, so to speak.

As I attended a strong Bible Teaching Church, I was led to join the leadership team for Women's Ministry. After serving close to four years, I began to feel a nudge in my heart to ask about the teaching of the Baptism of the Holy Spirit, since I was made aware that this wasn't mentioned in all the time I was attending. To shorten the story, I was given "the boot" from the leadership for not agreeing with their theology on the subject. That caused me to seek God's Word even more diligently. Again, I understood that I wasn't heading to hell if I didn't speak in tongues. I just knew I was desperate for everything God had for me, and I wanted to be free from the effects of betrayal on my life. Up to this point, I was a confessing Christian for nineteen years and was still miserable deep inside my soul. On the outside, I was serving with a smile. I may have been fooling everyone except God. I was on a personal mission to get to the heart of My Father regarding this Baptism of Spirit and Fire. I prayed and looked for several writings on this subject and was only going to believe the Scriptures that confirmed my research. I prayed fervently against all deception. I was sick and tired of being deceived!

By far, the most influential and thorough book I've ever read on the subject was written by Dave Roberson, entitled, *The Walk of The Spirit – The Walk of Power*. The entire book can be downloaded for free online. (daveroberson.org) I bought a printed copy so I could make notes along the way.

Every question I ever asked myself in the battle to believe this gift was for me (and every believer for that matter) is answered in that book! It wasn't just a good read. It proved to be a valuable resource. I humbly suggest it be kept on your reference shelf if you choose to buy a hard copy.

Going through *The Walk of the Spirit – The Walk of Power* is like one giant Bible study on understanding this phenomenal gift of praying in tongues. It is loaded with and supported by God's Word throughout. I knew the author personally as the humblest person one could ever meet. It was truly an honor and privilege to observe the fruit of the Spirit in his life. His demonstration of a life in Christ Jesus was a testimony from which the book was birthed. He is now enjoying the fruit of His labor in Heaven. I don't know if there will be several languages in Heaven, but the Bible says the language will be pure, that all may call on the name of the Lord, to serve Him with one accord *(Zephaniah 3:9)*. So, it doesn't seem we would need the gift of tongues in Heaven. But on the earth, it can be used to battle with the unseen realm while we are here.

True humility empowers us by God's grace to seek after His heart in all things that pertain to life and godliness. The gift of speaking in tongues is no exception.

Again, if you are having thoughts such as, "Sounds crazy" or "That seems ridiculous," ask the Holy Spirit if those thoughts are from your own belief system or from His. Sit quietly, humble yourself, listen, and just see if the God who made you assures you that He wants you to win by praying in the Spirit; sweet mysteries that only He understands. I tried it, and it worked. It still works today, as God is the same yesterday, today, and forever.

Exercising faith is a choice, every minute of every day, in Jesus's mighty name.

Dave Roberson covers the gift of praying in tongues in detail but adds another important weapon that works for the believer, resulting in victory over the enemy. And that weapon is fasting. This weapon causes our soul to prosper because it involves dying to our fleshly desires, like food and drink. The flesh will scream, "I'll die if I don't eat!" Try it. Even if it is just skipping one meal in your day. Pray in the Spirit in place of eating that burger, fries, and shake. This is a discipline that takes time to develop. It is also a powerful way to humble ourselves. And remember what humility brings? You got it, God's grace.

Prayer with fasting will result in hearing God's voice clearly, and His grace will empower you to fast and pray. If you have a diagnosis that requires you to take food with medicine, obviously, take the food, but possibly in a smaller amount than usual. Also, sweets can **always** be fasted. The Holy Spirit will help you if your heart is truly wanting to draw closer and more intimately with Jesus.

All these weapons that prosper require faith toward God. There is an arsenal of weapons, such as The Name of JESUS, The BLOOD of JESUS, Declarations of the Living Word of God, and so many others. All these have been made available for the believer to access. These would be a great study for all who are reading this book. We can never know enough about our victory in Christ Jesus!

Father, thank you for the gift of Your Spirit! Fill us!! Immerse us as we choose to humble ourselves by praying in the Spirit and fasting. We die to leaning on our own understanding. Help us understand You and Your ways through Your Spirit in Jesus's name.

CHAPTER SEVEN

WHAT'S FAITH GOT TO DO WITH IT?

"He who believes in Me as the Scripture has said, 'out of his heart will flow Rivers of Living Water.' But this He spoke concerning the Spirit, whom those believing in Him, would receive; for the Holy Spirit was not yet given, because Jesus was not yet glorified" *(John 7:38,39 NKJV)*.

As I was dwelling on these words, the Holy Spirit reminded me of a time I was sitting quietly, imagining "rivers of living water" flowing out of my heart. He began to reveal to me that those rivers are the testimony of Jesus, flowing by His Spirit.

Whenever I hear and obey God's voice, He can use me to share His testimony on the earth. He will use anyone who hears and obeys Him. Our spiritual ears are open to hear Jesus clearly once the clutter is removed from our souls. Sin blocks our ears from God's voice. That is why He hates it so much. It is a wedge that separates us from Him. His Gospel of the Kingdom is simple. I began to write as the Holy Spirit reviewed how I could even be having a conversation with Him in that moment. Here is what I wrote, and I quote:

"Jesus was glorified when He rose from the grave and ascended to the Father. I (Holy Spirit) was sent by Them (The Father and Jesus) to the earth as mankind's teacher, helper, comforter, and counselor. I am here today to lead and guide humanity into all truth. I am the one who empowers you to overcome the darkness. I reveal to whosoever will hear the testimony of Jesus."

Holy Spirit then highlighted this Scripture verse to me:

Revelation says, "For the testimony of Jesus is the spirit of prophecy" *(Revelation 19:10 last part NKJV)*.

When we allow the Spirit of Prophecy to work through us, those on the receiving end will be divinely encouraged, edified, and exhorted.

I pray the following content will do just that for you. These words came from notes I wrote down while sitting still and meditating on John 7:38-39. I am not saying it is a "thus saith the Lord." I'm merely choosing to step out in faith because I love Him.

1 John 4:1 instructs us to test the spirits. I tested this as well. I encourage you to do the same.

These words blessed me, so I wanted to forward the blessing. If you have a relationship with Jesus and are open to receiving His love in this way, then I invite you to imagine the Father speaking to you personally as you read. It's all about faith, after all. Here is what I journaled:

> "Faith in Me allows your well of Living Water to remain full and bubbling over. I've said, 'Faith without works is dead'; therefore, to truly worship Me is to believe what I say. Believing me will fuel a lifestyle of worship. Showing Me you believe what I say to you, is to walk it out in obedience. When you do what I say, it is the highest form of worship. This brings Me great delight, My child. This is the only way to grow in the grace and knowledge of My Son, Jesus Christ. Allow Him to help you obey Me continually!
>
> They that worship Me, must worship Me in Spirit and in Truth. This is love's way. There is no other way to worship Me and be recognized as My true disciple. If you do not allow your faith in Me to operate in your life, then you will struggle with knowing that Jesus is on the inside of you. He is willing and well able to help you walk out My perfect will for your life. Keep your eyes on Me, and you won't give glory to your own works and abilities. It is I who brings you from faith to faith and glory to glory. My grace allows you to understand this.
>
> Do you really, truly, deeply believe that My Son is living inside of you? Do you, without reservation, believe you have the mind of Christ? When you became born again, born of the Spirit [which is the Spirit of Truth], this knowledge of My works was deposited into your spirit by faith. 'Faith comes by hearing and hearing by the Word of God.' It's all there in your beautiful, born-again spirit. What keeps this treasury of knowledge from being walked

in, is that part of you that has yet to be renewed. Your cluttered belief system, your will, your emotions, and your voices that have been programmed according to your life's past experiences.

Before receiving My Son into your heart, you weren't able to fully understand why you thought the way you did, other than by human reasoning. This is why the Scribes and Pharisees hated Jesus so much. He had something they didn't. He taught truth with authority they didn't have. They only had head knowledge and needed to be born of the Spirit to understand the things that Jesus spoke of. My Son had the words of life for their spirit. They needed to receive Him, to receive life. The religious leaders took pride in memorizing the Torah from their youth. They were betrayed by their human logic, always learning but never able to come to a knowledge of the truth *(2 Timothy 3:7 NIV)*. Pride was at the root of the betrayal.

Pride is in opposition to My name. I will only give grace to the humble. It's pride that causes human reasoning to voice its own opinion. Pride doesn't care what others have to say. It stems from selfish desires that war within the human heart.

My Son spoke what He only heard me say. Jesus said, 'Whoever speaks on their own does so to gain personal glory, but he who seeks the glory of the one who sent him is a man of truth; there is nothing false about him.' *(John 7:18 NIV)*.

Staying in My written Word will keep you focused on the prize of your high calling of Me in Christ Jesus. Remain steadfast in My love. Embrace and follow Me. Choose to live by every word that proceeds out of My mouth.

In Me there is victory! You are more than a conqueror through My Son. You were made to succeed. We desire to have it said about you, 'Well done, My good and faithful servant'!

My Spirit is in the process of transforming you by renewing your thinking. He was sent to convince you that you have been freed from your past mindsets and that you now have the mind of Christ. This is a lifelong process of transformation, but a time is coming when you will see Me as I AM, in all My glory! You are called to reflect My glory! That is why I ordained from the foundation of the world for Jesus to live inside of you!

How willing are you to surrender to My glory? The purpose I have for you is to radiate My goodness and mercy toward others; to love them by obeying what I tell you to do and how to do it. When you are obeying Me, I know you really love Me. It takes sacrifice. It takes a free will, choosing to crucify your old nature. Your old mindsets will manifest behavior in opposition to My kindness, love, and mercy.

Everything belongs to Me, but out of My love for you, I have given you a free will. It is all yours. I gave it to you so you could choose to walk in the freedom I have set before you. It was for freedom that you were set free *(Galatians 5:1)*.

When your belief system is renewed, then your old behaviors will be gone along with the old belief system that fueled them. Love will abound richly in all the choices you make. This is My Kingdom! This is what My Glory looks like. I've called you personally to be holy as I AM HOLY!

As I said earlier, 'Out of your heart [belly], shall flow Rivers of Living Water ...' If you will allow those Rivers to flow by My Spirit, I will restore life back into the areas of your soul that were affected by betrayal. I will be glorified in your transformation. You are My treasure, My pearl of great price. My Son left everything to come to the Earth and pay the price for your eternity, My beloved. You are worth it. I look forward to our eternity together. Ezekiel 47:9 says, '… where the river flows, everything will live'" *(NIV). End quote.*

These notes were written as though the Father was sitting in a chair next to me, just sharing His heart. He may speak differently to you; in a way you understand more clearly. I pray He spoke to you by His Spirit, as you read the words above.

The Bible says that we must believe in the love that God has for us, for when we abide in this LOVE, we are literally abiding in God! *(1 John 4:16).*

Now that is a freedom, I dare say we would enjoy experiencing for all eternity! To be one with God! I ask again then, what's faith got to do with it?

Everything. Period. If we want to be free from the effects of betrayal on our lives, we must abide in His love. Faith in God overcomes every false way. In other words, faith in God challenges every reader to believe what Jesus says is true. "All things are possible to him who believes" *(Mark 9:23 RSV).*

I like to put it this way: Faith does the dance in advance, out of our romance with the King.

King Jesus is coming for a pure and spotless bride. May we be well-prepared and adorned to be wed on that day. In Him, we will remain forever, as one.

May His Grace richly abound and cause your soul to prosper in every way, in Jesus's Name. Amen. To God be ALL the GLORY!

www.ingramcontent.com/pod-product-compliance
Lightning Source LLC
Chambersburg PA
CBHW070548090426
42735CB00013B/3110